TRANSCENDING
EXILE *Conrad*
Nabokov
I.B. Singer

Asher Z. Milbauer

TRANSCENDING
EXILE *Conrad*
Nabokov
I.B. Singer

University Presses of Florida
FLORIDA INTERNATIONAL UNIVERSITY PRESS
MIAMI

Permission from the following publishers to quote from copy-righted material is gratefully acknowledged: McGraw-Hill Book Company, *Mary* and *Poems and Problems* by Vladimir Nabokov; New Directions Publishing Corporation, *The Real Life of Sebastian Knight* by Vladimir Nabokov; Farrar, Straus and Giroux: *Shosha* (copyright © 1978 by Isaac Bashevis Singer), *The Slave* (copyright © 1962 by Isaac Bashevis Singer), *Enemies, A Love Story* (copyright © 1972 by Isaac Bashevis Singer).

University Presses of Florida is the central agency for scholarly publishing of the State of Florida's university system, produc-ing books selected for publication by the faculty editorial com-mittees of Florida's nine public universities. Orders for books published by all member presses of University Presses of Flor-ida should be addressed to University Presses of Florida, 15 NW 15th Street, Gainesville, FL 32603.

Library of Congress Cataloging in Publication Data

Milbauer, Asher Z.
    Transcending exile.

    Bibliography: p.
    Includes index.
    1. Fiction—Exiled authors—History and criticism.
2. Fiction—20th century—History and criticism.
3. Conrad, Joseph, 1857–1924—Criticism and interpretation.
4. Nabokov, Vladimir Vladimirovich, 1899–1977—Criticism and interpretation. 5. Singer, Isaac Bashevis, 1904–   —Criticism and interpretation. I. Title.
PN495.M54 1985   809.3   84–22104
ISBN 0-8130-0815-8 (alk. paper)

for Luba

*How shall we sing the Lord's
song in a strange land?*

Contents

Acknowledgments

I wish to express my wholehearted appreciation and gratitude to Professor Edward Alexander for being my guide and teacher.

I am indebted to Professors Richard A. Dwyer, Malcolm Griffith, Donald M. Kartiganer, Willis Konick, Donald G. Watson, Elie Wiesel for their assistance, advice, scholarly insight, and patience.

It is difficult to overstate the kindness and generosity of Mr. and Mrs. Leo Jacobs, whom I thank for all their help.

For constant encouragement and moral support I wish to thank Leah Alexander, Gary and Lynda Brock, Frederica and Philip Gross, Michael Levine, David and Marsha Mesher, and Harold and Mildred Rosenbaum.

The timely assistance I received from the Memorial Foundation for Jewish Culture is greatly appreciated.

Many thanks to Elaine Dillashaw for being at once typist and friend.

I owe my deepest gratitude to my wife, Luba, my parents Tzviya and Yishayahu, my brothers, Yaakov and Zeev, for always being there.

Preface

Some time ago I came across Joseph Conrad's definition of a transplant as someone who is "uprooted" and whose "state of existence" is "unnatural." The fact that Conrad himself was an exile lends authority to his definition. Most of the questions he raises about exile hinge on the word *unnatural*. What precisely does it mean? How is an "unnatural" state of existence different from a natural one? Is there any possibility of transcending the "unnatural" state of existence? Can a transplant ever achieve a state of existence that will be natural? What are the consequences of unnatural living? Reading Conrad, I became aware that the answers to these questions were vital to one's understanding of his fiction; moreover, Conrad's own survival as an intellectual in exile depended upon his finding plausible answers in his life to the problems of transplantation that he constantly poses in his fiction.

Helped by my own experiences with exile, I felt intuitively that Conrad's preoccupation with the problems of exile might be shared by other transplanted writers. My efforts to see affinities between the Polish-English artist and other exiled authors led me to I. B. Singer, with whom I share a common native language—Yiddish. At first sight, the only similarity that exists between these two writers is that both are functioning in a new and alien environment. But the similarities, as I came to recognize in the course of my further readings, do not stop at this point; they run not only through the biographical data of Singer and Conrad but through many of their works, which can be analyzed comparatively. The most striking similarities are found on the thematic and structural levels of their novels and stories. The majority of the two writers' books provide a behavioral analysis through fiction of transplanted characters who struggle for survival in a surrounding unfamiliar to them. More often than not, their efforts to transcend and survive exile end in death, either physical or spiritual.

My long-standing interest in Vladimir Nabokov, whose language and country were once mine as well, and who became a successful artist notwithstanding the fact that he wrote in a foreign tongue in a country thousands of miles from his native soil, prompted my decision to include this Russian colossus in exile with the Polish Conrad and Jewish Singer. The study of Nabokov's fiction strengthened the hypothesis that I formed while reading Conrad and Singer. Many of Nabokov's books deal with the problems that attracted the attention of the other two transplanted authors; and their characters very often share a common fate.

Reading such works as *Mary, The Real Life of Sebastian Knight, Pnin, Shosha, The Slave, Enemies, A Love Story,* "Heart of Darkness," *Under Western Eyes,* and *Victory,* and keeping in mind the sometimes scarce and sometimes plentiful biographical information available on the authors of these works, I concluded that a substantial part of this fiction is deeply rooted in private and highly personal experiences. In the following chapters I address myself primarily to this autobiographical aspect of their writing.

My personal and professional interest in transplantation in general and literary transplantation in particular directed my attention to writers with the ability to write in an acquired language. Native speakers often have enormous difficulties writing clearly in their own language, though it comes to them naturally and they use it reflexively. Why, then, one might ask, would a foreigner undertake such a painful and exhaustive endeavor as mastering a new language in order eventually to make it into a medium of his art, a means to reach an audience, an instrument of intellectual survival? Nabokov and Conrad adopted the language of their countries of exile. I. B. Singer, for his part, has never written in English; his language always was and remains Yiddish.

Can even those who do not acquire the language of the country they live in be grouped under the label of transplants? Does the "rule" admit exceptions like I. B. Singer? The chapter on the Yiddish writer will show that even though Singer has never shifted to using English, he nevertheless belongs to the unique group of transplanted authors. The reasons for this exception, as we shall see, depend on Singer's particular experience and on his concern for a transplanted nation (the Jewish people), whereas Conrad and Nabokov create more personalized and individualized—though representative—characters.

My study of literary transplantation is limited to three exiles to the West who gained professional prominence only after they had left their homelands. Although aware of other modern exiled artists, I intentionally confine my study to Conrad, Nabokov, and I. B. Singer. There are two main reasons for doing so. First, my background, personal experiences, and knowledge of languages allow me a more intimate, yet not less objective, treatment of these three East European authors. Second, the discussion of the lives and works of other exiled groups would significantly alter the format and objective of my study. To subject these others to a superficial analysis will not do them justice. Given the complexity of the problem of literary transplantation, they deserve more. A fair treatment of other exiled groups of writers would require additional studies that address themselves to the peculiarities of this or another group of transplanted artists. I hope, however, that the answers to the numerous questions posed by transplantation emerging in the process of my analyses of the fiction and biographical data of Conrad, Nabokov, and I. B. Singer will be applicable not only to these authors but also to the lives and works of others artists, who "voluntarily" or by force have sought refuge and creative freedom outside the boundaries of their homelands.

The nature of my study and its direction led me to the decision to employ the well-tested method of traditional literary analysis rather than the more fashionable, albeit often useful, approaches practiced by formalists and structuralists. This resolution, coupled with the focus of my research on the development and growth of Conrad, Nabokov, and Singer through exile, prompted the final arrangement of the book. The short introductory chapter on Conrad isolates the most important issues associated with literary transplantation, thus creating a paradigm according to which the lengthier and more detailed discussions of Nabokov and Singer are organized. I intend to make clear that the Polish writer's literary career as well as the predicaments of his exile— as opposed to those of Nabokov and Singer—were shaped by different historical, social, and literary circumstances. A writer of an earlier generation, cofounder of modernism, and witness to the tragic destiny of his native Poland, Conrad, it is important to remember, does not share Nabokov's and Singer's experiences in the two events that have drastically changed the course of humankind's history and resulted in a massive displacement of entire segments of population: the communist Revolution in Russia and the Holocaust. Conrad's involvement with the problems of exile is less "obsessive" and intensely personal; it is not often easily discernible; yet it is always there. The introductory nature of the first chapter accounts for the exclusion of many works by Conrad, most notably *Nostromo*, which both directly and indirectly concerns exile. Instead, I will focus my attention on "Amy Foster," a short story that I consider to be a classic study of transplantation.

Prolific as the Russian and Jewish writers are, I have chosen to limit discussion to what I consider to be the most representative novels by each author; I will also refer to their short stories and, in the case of Nabokov, to his poetry as well, because they serve as important transitions between the larger canvases of these authors.

In regard to the chapter on Nabokov, it seemed natural to start with *Mary*, his first Russian novel, which embodies many significant elements that go into his later works. I have selected *The Real Life of Sebastian Knight* to follow *Mary* not only because it marks the end of Nabokov's European exile but, most important, because it is the first novel by the Russian writer created in English. *Pnin* concludes my treatment of Nabokov's fiction, since it aptly illustrates the relationship between the shift from one language to another and the consideration of a new audience—a relationship that any transplanted author must face on his way to transcending Conrad's "unnatural state of existence."

Singer's treatment of exile and literary transplantation differs from those of Conrad and Nabokov. Like the Polish and the Russian authors, he examines the nature of an individual's experiences of exile; unlike them, Singer deals not only with an individualized, though representative, character but also with an entire exiled nation. A Jewish writer's task is indeed formidable; after all, the history of his people is the history of exile. It is not surprising, then, that Singer, in his constant search for the right ways to transcend his own transplanted state as well as that of the Jewish people, often turns into an adventurous traveler in time and space. The answers to the vital issues of Jewish survival may be found, Singer implies, only if one can establish an unequivocal link between the causes and effects of the biblical exile and those associated with more recent displacements of his people. Singer's resolutions are both straightforward and ambivalent—they may vary from work to work. Because of this, I came to recognize that the chronological arrangement of the material used in the Nabokov section will not suffice in Singer's case. Instead, the first book I discuss is *Shosha*, a recent autobiographical novel that encompasses the most representative traits of Singer's entire literary production and reflects his often ambiguous responses to exile and literary transplantation. My readings of *The Slave*, a genuine laboratory of exile, and *Enemies, A Love Story*, an intricate study in ambiguity, follow the *Shosha* segment and help to explain why a son of a rabbi and a product of the European Enlightenment finds it so difficult to resolve the often insurmountable problems of Jewish existence and exile.

All my queries about literary transplantation will converge on the central question of the book: How does anyone, particularly an intellectual, survive exile and transcend his "unnatural state of existence"? What are the means that writers offer to their characters to stay alive under the circumstances of transplantation? Finally, what is the relation between these fictional inventions and the strategies employed by Conrad, Nabokov, and I. B. Singer to survive as writers and human beings?

One

JOSEPH CONRAD

Marginal Existence

*I am a transplanted being. Transplanted! I
ought to call myself uprooted—an unnatural
state of existence; but man is supposed to
stand anything.*
Heyst in *Victory*

*Ah! He was different; innocent of heart, and
full of good will, which nobody wanted, this
castaway, that like a man transplanted into
another planet, was separated by an immense
space from his past and by an immense
ignorance from his future.*
Dr. Kennedy in "Amy Foster"

An acquaintance with the lives and fiction of transplanted writers suggests that the origins of their literary creations will be, in part, biographical. Comparing their memoirs, interviews, and personal reminiscences with their novels and stories, one discovers the only slightly camouflaged fact that many events in these writers' lives found an easy passage into their fiction. Nabokov, according to his own admission, endows many of his characters with his own traits. I. B. Singer, for his part, repeatedly announces that he is all of his characters. The tendency to fictionalize their lives is indeed a distinctive feature of these writers.

Joseph Conrad powerfully illustrates this tendency. Like Na-

1

bokov and Singer, he readily acknowledges that his novels and stories are very autobiographical. In 1925, Arthur Symons, an acquaintance and contemporary, published a study of Conrad that is invaluable for its inclusion of some of his previously unknown letters. In one we read: "I know that the novelist lives in his work. He stands there, the only reality in an invented world, amongst imaginary things, happenings and people. Writing about them, he is only writing about himself. Every novel contains an element of autobiography and this can hardly be denied, since the creator can only explain himself in his creation."[1] What Conrad is trying to tell Symons in this letter is perfectly clear, and yet he finds it necessary to modify and amplify the above in his memoir, *A Personal Record.* Reproducing the statement word for word, he adds that his "disclosure" was not "complete." The writer, he says, "remains, to a certain extent, a figure behind the veil; a suspected rather than a seen presence— a movement and a voice behind the draperies of fiction."[2]

Sincere as these pronouncements may be, Conrad thinks that he owes the reader more than just general statements about the relationship of his work to his life. In the second half of the memoir, he straightforwardly admits that his literary production is inseparable from his personal life and that, when discussed or analyzed, they should not be divorced. "A writer of imaginative prose (even more than any other sort of artist)," Conrad asserts, "stands confessed in his works."[3] One can hardly accuse Conrad of being merely a confessional writer, yet his acknowledgment of his presence in his work as well as his admission of how many highly personal feelings and motivations enter his creative process cannot be lightly dismissed. The clues to a better understanding of the sensibility and genius of Conrad lie in his fiction, where he "stands confessed." True also of Nabokov and Singer, this often submerged entanglement of fact and fiction, past and present, reality and fantasy is one of the major characteristics of transplanted writers.

Conrad never tires of reiterating the fact that he can write only about things he himself experienced or came in touch with personally. Almost every Author's Note points this out. He writes about what he knows best; he brings to his fiction his knowledge of himself and narrates in a fictional form events from his life;

he generously endows his characters with his own traits, both weaknesses and strengths. The quandaries that accompanied Conrad's personal life and were behind his restlessness and inability to settle anywhere for long become the themes and major ingredients of his writings. Many of his characters, as Gustav Morf points out in his excellent Jungian study of Conrad's works and life, are projections of the writer's own subconscious.[4] While making his hero go through the process of "individuation," Conrad manages to rid himself of the numerous problems generated by exile.

Exiles in general and intellectuals in particular secretly fear being misunderstood. They are constantly alert lest what they say might be comprehended in a different way than intended. Aware of the wide gap that exists between their sensibility and mentality and those of the people that surround them, they express these worries in different ways. Sometimes transplants are too wordy in stating their points; often they interrupt their discourse with questions like, "Do you understand?" or "Do you see what I want to say?" to ascertain that their listeners or readers are correctly perceiving their ideas and statements. The latter is especially true of Conrad. Conrad is always worried whether or not his characters are understood; if they are misunderstood, the author has no chance to be comprehended. Like his fictional characters—Marlow, Lord Jim, Yanko Goorall, Razumov, and Heyst, to name a few—the writer aspires to be clear and understood properly, a matter of utmost importance for him. The following passage from "The Secret Sharer" is representative: "As long as I know that you understand. . . . But of course you do. It's a great satisfaction to have got somebody to understand."[5] Marlow, Conrad's double and mouthpiece, when conveying the story of his quest for Kurtz in "Heart of Darkness," occasionally interrupts his narrative to make sure that his listeners are still following him. His questions, "Do you see him? Do you see the story?"[6] can be paraphrased into Conrad's own questions, "Do you *see* me? Do you understand *me*?" To be fully comprehended is important to Conrad in order to gain self-knowledge and, consequently, to be able to face his exiled reality; moreover, he is eager to be understood by an audience whose way of life, modes of thinking, and sensibilities may be quite different from those of a Polish aristocrat, a seafarer, a cosmopolitan, in short, an exiled intellectual.

Many of Conrad's novels and stories illustrate the fact that exile and transplantation generate misunderstandings and breaks in communication. Without understanding and communication, life often becomes unbearable, void of any meaning, a burden frequently removed only by death. Exile in most of the Polish-English writer's works is indeed synonomous with death. The lives of Conrad's narrators, his doubles and mouthpieces, are spared. This naturally enables them to tell the tragic stories of exile; and Conrad, in his turn, translates these accounts into art and thereby transcends his exile. We shall see this tendency at work in the novels and stories of Nabokov and Singer. Yet, whereas these writers finally find that intellectual and artistic strength to spare the lives of their characters in their later works and offer them strategies to transcend exile, Conrad, for his part, remains deadly cruel to his main heroes. His characters take with them into their graves the unbearable problems of transplanted existence (which are also the exiled author's problems), leaving behind their creator, relieved and cleansed, and now able to move to the creation of still another novel or story.

After exhausting all the opportunities of a twenty-year-long seafaring career, a life of exile in its own right, Conrad turned to writing as the means to transcend his "earthly" transplanted state. Only by transforming the art of seamanship into the art of imaginative literature, by reliving his years of worldwide travel and turning the memories of his adventures into a "feat of memory," a "record of experience" that "in its facts, in its inwardness and its outward colouring, begins and ends in myself,"[7] can Conrad survive the hardships of his exile. Art for Conrad becomes *the* means of survival.

Conrad's entire literary creation reflects his perpetual efforts to come to terms with his own transplanted existence. A detailed interpretation of Conrad's short story "Amy Foster" as well as somewhat shorter reviews of "Heart of Darkness," *Under Western Eyes*, and *Victory* will illustrate this assertion.

Conrad completed the writing of "Amy Foster" on 18 June 1901. By this time he was already a novelist of good standing. The creation of such masterpieces as "Heart of Darkness," *Lord*

Jim, and *The Nigger of the "Narcissus"* had secured his place in English literature. However, critics' initial reactions to this story were unfavorable. Quiller-Couch expressed the generally accepted view of this short piece, calling it "not worthy" of the author of "Youth."[8] This contemptuous reception of the story did not, however, discourage other literary critics from returning to it and discovering it to be a richly suggestive tale.

Most critics believe "Amy Foster" to be a spiritual autobiography that reflects alienation, frustration, and the heightened sense of the tragedy of exile shared by the author and his protagonist Yanko Goorall.[9] A few, in their effort to dismiss this thesis as the central concern of the story, try, first to trace its sources and then to establish the significance the story might have had in modifying Conrad's outlook "on love and marriage."[10] Robert J. Andreach comes closest to answering the questions posed by the author, yet he stops short, as does the narrator of "Amy Foster," when he finds himself in front of insurmountable mysteries and the unspeakable truths the story contains.[11] Exile, indeed, can often be a frightening experience, and it is this experience that underlies "Amy Foster."

The story compels attention for several reasons. Joseph Conrad rarely failed to comment on his novels or stories in the Author's Notes that invariably accompany them. In the 1926 edition of Conrad's *Complete Works,* "Amy Foster" shares a volume with three other short stories: "Typhoon," "Falk: A Reminiscence," and "Tomorrow." While he supplies the reader with some background and biographical material on the last three stories, all Conrad has to say about "Amy Foster" is that it was published in the *Illustrated London News.* The writer intentionally (and conspicuously) omits detailed comments on "Amy Foster." In manuscript form, the story had initally been called "The Husband"; before its completion it was renamed "The Castaway"; finally it was published as "Amy Foster." It is peculiar that by changing the title of the story, Conrad does, in a way, shift the emphasis from his main protagonist to his wife-to-be and endows her with the name Amy Foster, a name whose connotations have far-reaching consequences.

"Amy Foster" can be regarded as a classical study of exile. That Conrad chooses to have a physician, that is, a man of science, as a narrator lends credence to this claim. Even before letting the narrator start his recreation of a mysterious happening, the writer finds it necessary to characterize him as follows: "His intelligence is of a scientific order, of an investigating habit, and of that unappeasable curiosity which believes that there is a particle of a general truth in every mystery."[12] In addition, by telling us that Dr. Kennedy "has the talent of making people talk to him freely, and an inexhaustible patience in listening to their tales" (p. 106), Conrad establishes the narrator's reliability. Kennedy is thus endowed by the author with all the qualities that make him a credible storyteller. Although a scientist, an investigator, a psychologist, a good listener, in short, a man who has the ability to understand as well as to make others "see," Dr. Kennedy is predestined to fail to grasp the meaning and essence of human nature and existence. He will not be able to penetrate the complicated mechanism of Yanko's tragedy, although he very perceptively identifies its source as "arising from irreconcilable differences and from the fear of the Incomprehensible that hangs over our heads—over our heads" (p.108).

The plot of "Amy Foster" is simple. Yanko is the only survivor of a shipwrecked German vessel, *Herzogin Sophia-Dorothea*, which was carrying hundreds of Polish peasant emigrants to America. The ship sinks under quite mysterious circumstances when it is anchored in Eastbay. (I will return to this mystery in my later discussion of Conrad's attitude toward Russia and Germany.) Since the ship disappears during the night, and the tragic fate of the vessel is not generally known, the populace of the nearby English village fails to see any connection between the vanished ship and the wild, outlandish-looking man who is seen roaming about in their village. Yanko's strange appearance strikes terror into the hearts of the English peasants. Upon encountering him, they treat the Polish castaway with total disrespect and indeed exceptional cruelty.

After being harassed by a coachman, humiliated by women, chased by children, Yanko finally finds himself trapped in a pigsty belonging to a Mr. Smith. The latter does not know how to deal with the situation; neither is he able to calm down his hysterical wife, who urges him to get rid of this unwelcome visitor. The only person who shows compassion toward Yanko is Amy

Foster, the Smith's dull and unpretentious maid. A day later, another landowner, Mr. Swaffer, known in the village for his eccentricities as well as for his weakness for the exotic, agrees to take Yanko into his house. Yanko becomes a servant to the Swaffers; after saving the life of the old man's granddaughter, he is rewarded by a patch of land and a little house of his own. Although he is "accepted" by the Swaffers, Yanko remains a pariah in the village, despised by everyone. Yet his now minimal financial independence allows him to marry and establish himself. Amy Foster, the first person to show compassion for him, becomes Yanko's wife. A year later, Amy gives birth to a son, a joyous occasion that also marks the beginning of the deterioration of Yanko and Amy's relationship. Yanko wants to raise Little Johnny the way he was brought up in the Carpathian Mountains; he is eager to teach his son Polish as well as his native folklore. Finally, when he becomes sick, Amy abandons Yanko to die in their cold house. Dr. Kennedy, after numerous attempts to establish the correct diagnosis of Yanko's illness, names heart failure as the cause of death. Dr. Kennedy may be wrong medically, but his intuition is correct—Yanko's heart has "failed" because it has been transplanted. In this apparently simple story, Conrad straightforwardly raises all the problems that accompany transplantation. This short piece turns into a paradigm of his work. The essence of exile and the problems of language are central points in the author's concern.

Exile determined Conrad's life. His first experiences with it go back to his childhood. Conrad's father, Apollo Korzeniowski, was a Polish patriot and nationalist who devoted his entire life to the struggle against the tzarist autocracy under whose reign Poland existed for many years. As one of the leaders of the 1861 insurrection, he was sent into exile to Vologda, a godforsaken Russian town. His wife, Ewelina, and his four-year-old son, Joseph, accompanied him into exile. In 1865, unable to cope with the hardships of their life, Ewelina died, followed by her husband's death four years later. At the age of eleven, Conrad was taken into the care of his maternal uncle, Tadeusz Bobrowski. Exile deprived Conrad of his parents. Never could he forgive Russia for its colonial policies in his native land. His overt hatred of Russia is a prevalent theme in many of his books.

The Russian exile was only Conrad's first encounter with the "unnatural state of existence."[13] At the age of seventeen, he himself went into exile in France; four years later he moved to England. He knew French well; his social connections there were excellent. As a result, his French period of exile did not present many problems to the future author. Life in England was different, though. The young man did not know English; his financial resources were meager; he had no friends to rely on. He did not find the British people hospitable, yet he made up his mind to succeed as an Englishman. Exile in England confronted Conrad with manifold problems.

In addition to the problem he faced as an exile, Conrad was constantly haunted by feelings of guilt and remorse for leaving behind his trouble-ridden country. This guilt and the complex of betrayal stayed with him always. Voices from Poland were always pursuing him, beckoning the lost son to return to his motherland. But to be under the yoke of the Russian oppressor was not a choice that he could voluntarily make. He decided to succeed as an Englishman, never forgetting, though, that he was born a Pole with all the consequences this heritage might have for him and his writing. To survive in exile, Conrad had to learn how to balance his past and present. To become "one of them" would have meant death; to give in totally to the claims of the past would have meant death as well. Art became Conrad's means of establishing an equilibrium between his past and his present experience.

"Amy Foster" synthesizes Conrad's problems in exile. It is a story of an extremely private nature, which is why Conrad never commented on it in detail. The importance of this story to Conrad's personal and professional life is underscored by his "sole extant Polish letter of almost three years"[14] to his namesake, the historian Joseph Korszeniowski. In part, this missive reflects Conrad's constant attempts to come to grips with being a Pole in England. He writes in rather firm terms that he has never forgotten his origins, that he will always be aware of his Polish heritage.

In "Amy Foster," the writer's main preoccupation is with language and the essence of exile, the two elements of transplanted existence that, as we will see, are also given close and constant attention in Singer's and Nabokov's literary creation. Students of Conrad know about the writer's long-standing concern with English. Conrad did not have the advantage of an English governess and a Cambridge education, as Nabokov did, to help him master the language which was to become his medium of expression. It was his father who first exposed Joseph to English literature. Yet, unlike Nabokov's father, who read to his son in English, Apollo read Dickens to his son in translation. Though Apollo was a translator of Shakespeare and knew English well, he did not impart this knowledge to his son. It was more important to him that Joseph master his native tongue.

Conrad recalls in his *Personal Record* that prior to his arrival in England at age twenty-one he knew no more than six English words.[15] His first contact with the English language took place during his travels in Europe at the age of sixteen with his tutor, whose mission it was to dissuade Joseph from becoming a seaman.[16] Conrad was first spoken to in English in Marseille. He remembered this moment with elation: "I heard myself addressed in English from the deck of the British ship, *James Westoll*—the speech of my secret choice, of my future, of long friendships, of the deepest affection, of hours of toil and hours of ease, and of solitary hours too, of books read, of thoughts pursued, of remembered emotions—of my very dreams! And if I dare not claim it aloud as my own, then, at any rate, the speech of my children."[17]

Conrad's formal education was supplanted by less formal learning aboard English ships. His first teachers were not the polished professors of English at Cambridge but the rough seamen of the North Sea. In his brilliant essay "Poland Revisited," he talks about his first years of apprenticeship to the English language:

> The North Sea was to me something unforgettable, something much more than a name. It had been for some time the schoolroom of my trade. On it, I may safely say, I had learned, too, my first words of English. A wild and stormy abode, sometimes, was that confined, shallow water academy of seamanship from which I launched myself on the wide oceans. My teachers had been the sailors of the Norfolk shore; coastmen with steady eyes, mighty limbs, and gentle voices; men of very few words, which at

least were never bare of meaning. Honest, strong, steady men, sobered by domestic ties, one and all, as far as I could remember.[18]

In addition to these rough yet kindhearted teachers, Conrad drew his profound knowledge of the English language from his readings of Shakespeare, Byron, Trollope, Mill, and other British writers. Conrad's decision to write in English rather than Polish or French puzzled many. The writer explains his decision himself. In the Author's Note to his memoir, *A Personal Record*, Conrad recalls a conversation with his friend Hugh Clifford about various linguistic problems, among them Conrad's decision to write in English. As a result of this conversation, Clifford concluded that Conrad was hesitant when confronted by the choice between French and English. Clifford later imparted this view to Walpole, who made it public. Conrad, for his part, grasped at that occasion to clarify the situation once and for all; and he did so in his memoir's Author's Note:

> The truth of the matter is that my faculty to write in English is as natural as any other aptitude with which I might have been born. I have a strange and overpowering feeling that it had always been an inherent part of myself. English was for me neither a matter of choice nor adoption. The merest idea of choice had never entered my head. And as to adoption—well, yes, there was adoption; but it was I who was adopted by the genius of the language, which directly I came out of the stammering stage made me its own so completely that its very idioms I truly believe had a direct action on my temperament and fashioned my still plastic character.
>
> It was a very intimate action and for that very reason it is too mysterious to explain.[19]

Conrad's decision to write in English is not as mysterious as he wants us to believe. Ten years separate his first literary endeavors from his arrival in England. During these long years, Conrad worked very hard to master the language. His determination to succeed in this country never abandoned him. He was also aware that Polish would be insufficient to render all the experiences that had happened so far away from his native land; Polish did not provide the linguistic variety to recreate his sea adventures. Although fluent in French, Conrad was exposed to it for only three years, and, as he once admitted to Garnett, had he decided to write in French he would have simply translated into it from English. It is only natural that Conrad, immersed for so long in the linguistic atmosphere of English, would write only in English. Leo Gurko, in his book *Joseph Conrad: Giant in Exile,* states that to write in English was the most logical choice Conrad could have made under the circumstances. "Of course," he asserts, "all the arguments why Conrad wrote in English, his third language in order of learning, can be simply resolved by the statement that he did so because he happened to be living in England at the time, was a British citizen and a captain in the British merchant marine, was speaking English and only English every day, and it would be extraordinary under the circumstances if he had chosen to write in any other language."[20] Conrad lends additional credence to Gurko's argument by stating, "All I can claim after all these years of devoted practice . . . is the right to be believed when I say that if I had not written in English, I would have not written at all."[21]

If English was for Conrad a language of professional endeavors, Polish, his native tongue, remained for him during his whole life the symbol of spiritual affinities for and national identity with his motherland. Many critics noticed how particular he was about not forgetting Polish; in part, Conrad was under pressure from his relatives and countrymen not to neglect his mother tongue. Tadeusz Bobrowski, his maternal uncle, never failed to comment on his nephew's language in the course of their long correspondence. The writer, for his part, did not disappoint his guardian. The latter, upon one of his meetings with Joseph, was pleased that he "had forgotten nothing of his Polish."[22] For Conrad, remembering his native tongue became a condition of preserving his integrity in exile as it prevented him from forgetting his past. His constant work to improve his English balanced this attempt to preserve his Polish; together these efforts secured the writer's intellectual survival.

In "Amy Foster," we see these two tendencies at work. On the one hand, Yanko is eager to master the English language, which, among other things, helps him to recreate the story of his past as well as to communicate these experiences to those who care to listen. On the other hand, Yanko does not want to give up his Polish language and culture, even though his persistence in maintaining them causes his estrangement from the village community.

In this particular story as well as in most works of Joseph Conrad, the problems of exile and the essence of a character's transplanted state always come under the author's scrutiny. Yanko Goorall is placed in an extreme situation: he is a castaway looked upon by the inhabitants of the English village as a creature from a different and uncivilized planet. Kennedy, the narrator, constantly provides the reader with vivid and impressive descriptions of the main protagonist; he never fails to underscore the fact that Yanko is out of place in his new surroundings:

> Here on the same road you might have seen amongst
> these heavy men a being lithe, supple and long-limbed,
> straight like a pine, with something striving upwards in
> his appearance as though the heart within him had been
> buoyant. Perhaps it was only the force of the contrast, but
> when he was passing one of the villagers here, the soles of
> his feet did not seem to touch the dust of the road. He
> vaulted over the stiles, paced these slopes with a long
> elastic stride that made him noticeable at a great dis-
> tance, and had lustrous black eyes. He was so *different*
> from the mankind around him that, with the freedom of
> movement, his soft—a little startled, glance, his olive
> complexion and graceful bearing, his humanity suggested
> to me the nature of a woodland creature. He came from
> there. (p. 111, my emphasis)

On yet another occasion, the doctor again stresses the polarity between Yanko and his new countrymen: "Ah! He was so different, innocent of heart, and full of good will, which nobody wanted, this castaway, that like a man transplanted into another planet, was separated by an immense space from his past and an immense ignorance from his future" (p. 132).

Yanko's foreignness and strangeness arouse no sympathy in the hearts of the villagers. He cannot help feeling "the hostility of his human surroundings" (p. 33). The only person who seems to exhibit a genuine interest in Yanko is Mr. Swaffer; but Conrad, when characterizing the old man, makes it clear that Mr. Swaffer is also a stranger among his own people, and he is known among them as a collector of outlandish specimens. Although Dr. Kennedy is unmistakably well disposed toward Yanko, he nevertheless takes interest in him for merely scientific reasons—he wants to see the results of his experiment of exile. Amy Foster's attitude to Yanko is still a different matter, which I will discuss later in this chapter.

Despite the hostility of his environment, Yanko does not give in to the despair. He wants to overcome his loneliness and alienation, the feelings of frustration and disappointment that are his inseparable companions. Like any exiled character, he is aware that the first step toward his new countrymen can only be made through language. Conrad had few difficulties in conveying Yanko's struggle to overcome the linguistic barriers in his country of exile; the writer had firsthand experience in this matter. Both the author and his protagonist know that once the language barrier is removed, the chances for spiritual and physical survival will be higher. Conrad is precise in describing this slow, painful process in "Amy Foster." First Yanko's English is "broken"; then it assumes the characteristics of "baby-talk." Later it "resembled curiously the speech of a young child" (p. 122). Yanko never stops in his efforts to improve his new language; and though he finally becomes fluent, his speech never loses "that singing, soft, and at the same time vibrating intonation that instilled a strangely penetrating power into the sound of the most familiar English words, as if they had been the words of an unearthly language" (p. 117). Though his English improves, Yanko's language is still strange, different, "unearthly."

Despite Yanko's nearly unlimited perseverance in his efforts to establish contact with his new countrymen, he nevertheless remains an outcast among them. No one seems to be interested in him. "He could talk to no one and had no hope in ever understanding anybody. It was as if these had been the faces of people from the other world—dead people" (p. 129). It takes years, indeed, for the villagers to get "used to see him. But they never became used to him" (p. 132). Conrad seems to go out of his way to underscore how different Yanko is from the English people; he is eager to locate these differences precisely; he wants to find the exact words to characterize them. He finally comes to the conclusion that Yanko's sensibility and imagination are what keep him apart from his new countrymen. The Englishmen, Conrad makes clear, lack these two features; and, as a result, they have no affinities with Yanko.

It is not only through language that Yanko seeks integration into the society. He changes many of his habits; he dresses like the rest of the villagers; he toils in the manner they do. But they demand more than Yanko can give. The peasants cannot stand to see Yanko crossing himself, exhibiting his adherence to the Catholic faith. His singing of Polish songs, his dancing of his native dances in the village pub gain no sympathy from those present. They beat, ridicule, and humiliate Yanko. When he speaks Polish the villagers turn their backs on him, showing their disrespect and lack of understanding for the foreigner. Yanko, in short, fails to make them understand who and what he is.

In his efforts to survive in England, Yanko goes as far as marrying one of the village girls. Naturally, his choice is Amy Foster, a dull and unpretentious woman, yet the only person who, according to the narrator, has enough imagination to see the positive qualities of her future husband. For Yanko, this marriage is his only hope of persuading the villagers as well as himself that he can succeed in England, that he can become "one of them." Yanko's desires, however, do not coincide with the overall design of the story, for the author knows better than that. To become "one of them," as we shall also see in the case of Kurtz, is identical to death.

Even at the beginning of the story, Conrad foreshadows Yanko's tragic fate. The episode that points to it is connected with Amy Foster. This girl, Conrad states,

> had never been heard to express a dislike for a single human being, and she was tender to every living creature. She was devoted to Mrs. Smith, to Mr. Smith, to their dogs, cats, canaries; and as to Mrs. Smith's gray parrot, its

peculiarities exercised upon her a positive fascination.
Nevertheless, when the outlandish bird, attacked by the
cat, shrieked for help in human accents, she ran out into
the yard stopping her ears, and did not prevent the crime.
(p. 109)

The image of an "outlandish" bird, encaged first and then brutally attacked from the outside, is Conrad's metaphor for Yanko
and his destiny.[23] To underscore the significance of this metaphor, as well as to direct the reader's attention back to it in the
course of the plot's development, Conrad, at different points in
the story, calls Yanko "a wild bird caught in a snare." The metaphorical cage of exile has also been used by both Nabokov and
Singer. Conrad's exiled hero, like theirs, is trying to find a way
out of the confinements of the cage. He thinks that marriage will
be his means to do so; but, instead, Yanko's relationship with
Amy turns out to be yet another snare.

The birth of a child is usually perceived by parents as a joyous
event. It may mark the inseparability of the father and mother;
it can be seen as a symbol of their spiritual affinity; it often
crowns their liaison. In Conrad's story, however, the birth of
Little Johnny begins Yanko's downfall. Despite Yanko's hopes, it
does not add to the balancing of the past and present. With Johnny's birth, Yanko's passions for the past are rekindled. The narrator often observes Yanko holding his son in his lap, singing to
him songs in Polish, reciting to the boy the prayers he was taught
in the house of his parents. He sees in the child "a man . . . to
whom he could sing and talk in the language of his country, and
show how to dance by and by" (p. 137). It is his past that Yanko
wants to recreate through the baby, since his past is rejected by
everything that represents the present. Yet again, this desire is
part of Conrad's irony. Yanko runs from one extreme to another
in search of ways to survive and transcend exile. Each means
death.

Amy Foster, for her part, is frightened when Yanko persists in
imparting his knowledge of the past and his love for the Polish
language, faith, and culture to Little Johnny. She becomes more
and more alienated from her husband. She fails to understand
him; she fails to help him when he needs her help the most. She

could have balanced Yanko's life and helped him to survive. Instead, when his mental powers and physical health worsen, Amy dissociates herself from Yanko's problems.

Dr. Kennedy describes Yanko's misery in detail. He often sees the castaway crying in the shade of the three pine trees that grow on the outskirts of the village, the trees that remind him of the vast pine forests in his native Poland. Frequently Yanko feels remorse and guilt for abandoning his parents who had to sell part of their estate to raise money for their son's passage to America. Yanko is indeeed trapped like a "wild bird" in a "snare." He has no way out, no means to free himself from the suffocating cage of exile. Conrad is not in a hurry to help his protagonist; instead, he is placing the problems of his own exile onto the shoulders of his countryman. Yanko collapses under this heavy burden and dies.

Had Yanko decided to blot out his past with its culture, language, faith, he would have become "one of them," that is, he would have stumbled into his spiritual death. Yet his new countrymen deny him even this option. England does not want to be his country. The most it can agree to, with some hesitation and reluctance though, is to be his foster country. Hence the surname of Amy and, consequently, the title of the story. On the other hand, when Yanko, rejected by his present, turns to his past and tries to preserve what is dear to him, he is threatened by another danger of exile—a too complete identification with the past that leads unavoidably to death.

"Amy Foster" makes quite clear the consequence of Conrad's experiments in exile. The complete, unqualified adaptation to and assimilation with an alien culture leads inevitably to spiritual extinction. Had Yanko assimilated into English society, his fate would have been no different from that of Al Cook in Nabokov's novel *Pnin* or Singer's American Jews, Rabbi Lampert, for example. To feed on one's past only, to live continually with thoughts directed only toward this past, leads to oblivion and death. Yanko's inability to separate himself from his previous experiences makes him unable to transcend exile. Yanko has his counterparts in the works of Nabokov and Singer. He shares the tragic fate of Anton Sergeyevich Podtyagin in *Mary*, of Sebastian Knight in *The Real Life of Sebastian Knight*, of Herman and Masha in *Enemies, A Love Story*. And yet we should recognize important distinctions. Both Nabokov and Singer try hard to find the means of survival not only for themselves but also for their characters. Conrad never gained the security and confidence of the Russian or the Yiddish writer. Nabokov has never felt guilty for leaving Russia; history has justified Singer's abandonment of Poland. Conrad, for his part, could never rid himself of the obsessive guilt over leaving the country for which his parents died. This remorse has also something to do with Conrad's being a Pole and an aristocrat. He often hated himself for his inability to come to terms with the two sides of his nature: his nationalism and his cosmopolitanism. His heart was in Poland; his mind was in England. He was bitter and angry about failing to achieve harmony between the two. The result of this perpetual inner struggle was his attitude toward his fictional characters, who, as we have seen from the discussion of "Amy Foster," suffer the same traumas. Since his heroes are close to him in their nature, he shows sympathy toward them but never comes to their rescue in times of trial. The writer is very worried about his own survival. And he does survive, yet only by transforming the fatal experiences of his characters into the triumphs of his own art.

The conclusions drawn from my reading of "Amy Foster" also apply to Conrad's other works, and in particular, to "Heart of Darkness." This short novel is the Polish-English writer's most intricate and controversial piece of writing. Similar to "Amy Foster," it is, to a great extent, a study of exile as well as yet another fictionalized biography of its author. It is not necessary to reiterate the oft-mentioned affinities between the adventures of Marlow and those of Conrad. It is well known that Conrad, assisted by his aunt, Poradowska, obtained the captaincy of a steamer in the Congo, that his experiences there were of the most impressive and dreadful nature, and that he barely survived the ordeal. Conrad's *Congo Diary* yields plentiful material to prove that "Heart of Darkness" is as much about Conrad's experience as it is about Marlow's. The novel is certainly not a product of the author's solipsism. In his Author's Note to the volume in which "Heart of Darkness" is included, Conrad writes that the novel is "as authentic and fundamental as 'Youth.'" He also calls it "an experience pushed a little (and only very little) beyond the actual facts of the case."[24]

Of even more interest in the Author's Note is Conrad's complete identification with Marlow. Their mentalities are the same; their ways of thinking are identical. "Of all my people," Conrad asserts, "he's [Marlow's] the one that has never been a vexation to my spirit. A most discreet, understanding man."[25]

Marlow, as Conrad's double and mouthpiece in "Heart of Darkness," is the one who wants to understand and be understood, who desires to see and be seen. His telling the story of Kurtz to listeners of different walks of life is his way of making things clearer to himself about a character who becomes an exile and who Marlow often calls "my shade" or "my shadow." Marlow thus betrays the affinities he shares with Kurtz. Conrad, in his turn, commits the story to paper, multiplying the three listeners into thousands upon thousands of readers who by the end of the narration should be able to recognize and understand the problems the author raises. Marlow, though frequently complaining how difficult it is to relate the occurrences from twenty years past, brings the story to its completion nevertheless. It is indeed a victory on his part; yet the real triumph lies in his pronouncement that "Kurtz made me see things."[26] Kurtz held up a mirror to Marlow in which the latter saw his own reflection. It expressed the results of Marlow's search for the truth of human nature. The mirror reflected horror stripped of outward appearances, the horror of exile and death.

Conrad foreshadows Kurtz's tragic fate even in the outset of the book. Marlow describes a map that he sees in the Parisian office of the company in charge of the Congo's conquest. The patches of yellow on the map mark his final destination. "'I was going into the yellow,'" he says, "'Dead in the centre. And the river was there—fascinating—deadly—like a snake. Ough!'" (p.56). This ominous exclamation, full of negative connotations, reverberates throughout the story and is transformed finally into a word that becomes its synonym: "The Horror! The Horror!"

What is it, then, that Kurtz makes Marlow see and understand? Is it something that Marlow knows all along yet lacks the courage to face? What is it that brings Kurtz to his death and, at the same time, spares Marlow's life? To answer these questions we have to retrace our steps to the beginning of the story where, we will find, both the answers and the intentions of the author are spelled out.

While getting ready for the trip to the Congo, Marlow has to undergo a medical examination. Trifling as it may seem, this incident throws light on Conrad's true intentions. The doctor, after completing the routine business of feeling Marlow's pulse, suddenly requests the captain's permission to measure his head. This strange entreaty takes Marlow by surprise; it seems bizarre and out of place. He agrees to the procedure nevertheless, asking in return for an explanation. The doctor's reasons betray his affinities with yet another doctor, that is, Kennedy, the narrator of "Amy Foster." He explains to Marlow that he wants to compare the measurements of his head before and after going to the Congo. From his experience, the doctor knows that the adventure of going to the Congo very often turns into a permanent affair. Those who go frequently stay there for many years and sometimes even for good. Going to the Congo, as we also find out from Marlow's observations, can mean becoming an exile. The results of the experience of becoming an exile, the doctor speculates, will indicate the changes in one's mind. " 'It would be,' " he says, " 'interesting for science to watch the mental changes of individuals, on the spot' " (p. 58). Taking his farewell from the astonished Marlow, he lifts a "warning forefinger" (p. 58) as if to admonish the captain to be careful and take good care of himself, lest he share the tragic destiny of his predecessors.

The doctor's inquisitiveness and curiosity, disregarded by Marlow as the eccentricities and whims of a feeble old man, turn, paradoxically, into his own inquisitiveness and curiosity upon his arrival in the Congo. When he observes all the waste around him, when he sees black men dying on the paths of darkness, when he notices all the squabbles among the white men, Marlow suddenly recalls the doctor's interest in "mental changes of individuals, on the spot" and feels as if he were "becoming scientifically interesting" (p. 72). Undergoing "mental changes" himself, Marlow becomes aware of his own growing "scientific" interest in the black continent and its inhabitants. Finally, his interest narrows to Kurtz and the changes this shade—apparition—shadow—has undergone during his self-imposed exile.

"Heart of Darkness" is a scientific experiment in "mental changes"—a study of exile with a tragic end. In my reading of "Amy Foster" I touched on a crucial problem around which any discussion of transplantation centers, namely, the question of belonging. Marlow, in his quest to understand Kurtz, finally narrows down the scope of this search to the same query. "'The thing was to know,'" he asserts, "'what he [Kurtz] belonged to, how many powers of darkness claimed him for their own'" (p. 116). For Kurtz is torn mainly between two powers—the power of his past and the power of his newly acquired present—in a conflict symbolized by the images of two women, his Intended and the native Congo Woman. But before discussing the two images, we need to review some facts about Kurtz himself.

In the course of the story, Conrad himself makes clear that Kurtz is indeed an extraordinary man, a "universal genius" (p. 73). He is a man of great talent and inimitable eloquence. We also find out that he is an artist. Marlow comes across a painting by Kurtz whose subject matter immediately arrests his attention and to which he alludes later in the book. In additon to being an artist, Kurtz is also a musician, a poet, a writer. Marlow is fascinated by the man's virtuosity with language. Regardless of the content of Kurtz's report to the International Society for the Suppression of Savage Customs, Marlow never tires in praising the quality of Kurtz's written word. He heaps one compliment upon another; he repeats himself on the subject many times, becoming wordy and somewhat redundant when he goes out of his way to underscore the intellectual attributes of the man he comes to admire. The reader feels that Marlow is afraid that he will not be understood, that he does not fully trust his listeners' abilities to see the genius of Kurtz. Kurtz's language, he says, "was eloquent, vibrating with eloquence (p. 117); his report "was a beautiful piece of writing" (p. 118); it possessed "the unbounded power of eloquence—of words—of burning noble words" (p. 118). Marlow wants the reader to understand that it is a shame that such a man, with such talents, should so tragically waste his life. If only Kurtz had used his genius properly, he would probably have survived. Yet for once, Conrad is not so much interested in Kurtz's survival as he is in making us see the real causes of his death. Cruel as Conrad is to Kurtz, nowhere else does he come so close to offering a character a means to survive and transcend his exile.

Kurtz's mortal sin is that he identifies completely with his newly acquired present. He leaves everything behind him and wastes his intellectual strengths in his efforts to become one with the natives of the Congo darkness. He identifies with them fully; he cannot break away from his new reality. Even when he finally decides to leave, he nevertheless orders the boat to turn around, and back he plunges into the darkness. Kurtz finally adopts the darkness with its culture, its rituals, its language, its mentality. He goes as far to participate in the "unspeakable rites" of the natives, which, according to Stephen Reid, consist "of human sacrifice and Kurtz's consuming a portion of the sacrificial victim."[27]

By divesting himself of his past completely, merging with the present and becoming "one of them," Kurtz assures his death. "Heart of Darkness" makes clear that there is a correct plane of existence even for an exile—a plane that integrates past and present, dream and fantasy, art and reality. This marginal existence is symbolically represented by a portrait of a woman Kurtz painted in the jungle. This art work combines two extremes: the world for which Kurtz's Intended stands and the world that is represented by the native woman. Conrad does not hide his intentions to juxtapose the images of these two women. There is a wide abyss between them, yet they want the same thing; they want Kurtz back. Both have claims upon him, but only Kurtz can choose. He finally gives preference to the native goddess, thus giving up the past to which his Intended beckons him. This act of Kurtz "secures" his death. But had he given in to the claims of the past, that is, to the world that is satisfied with lies and stagnation, he would have brought upon himself spiritual death. What, then, is the way out for a Conradian hero?

The answer lies in the implied meanings of Kurtz's portrait of a woman. Marlow describes it in this way: "I noticed a small sketch in oils, on a panel, representing a woman, draped and blindfolded, carrying a lighted torch. The background was sombre—almost black. The movement of the woman was stately, and the effect of the torchlight sinister" (p. 79). There is an inherent paradox in Kurtz's choice of his subject: why would a blindfolded woman need a lighted torch? The paradox conveys Conrad's view of exile: if a transplant fully identifies himself with the past, he is to die; if the complete identification is with the newly acquired present, the same fate awaits him. When creating his art, Kurtz intuitively knows the ways to transcend exile, namely, through art and intellect. Yet he chooses to pursue a different path. Only art, Conrad implies, can make the forces of darkness (the blindfold) and the powers of light (the torch) coexist on the same plane. Kurtz ignores the option of survival the writer offers him. Marlow, though, having learned from Kurtz's destructive experiences, picks up the torch whose light pushes aside the shadows of darkness, leaving him enough breathing space on the stage of life. Marlow's survival is Conrad's survival as well.

"Amy Foster," as Conrad's paradigmatic study of exile, defines many of the problems that accompany transplantation in general and Conrad's exile in particular. Yanko feels remorse and guilt for abandoning his native land. The theme of betrayal, though not outlined in much detail, is still something to which Conrad wants to attract his readers' attention. Another aspect of "Amy Foster," which is also presented in a veiled manner, is the writer's attitude toward Russia and Germany. First, there are the mysterious circumstances of the disappearance of the German ship loaded with Polish emigrants on their way to America; in additon the Coast Guard spots a steamer in the same area that is later blamed for the destruction of the German vessel. If we go along with Gustav Morf's theory that ships in Conrad's books often stand for countries,[28] it will not be hard to explain the appearance of this episode dealing with ships. Conrad often accused Russia and Germany of the destruction of Poland and the suppression of Polish nationalism. Conrad was also angry at England and France for standing aside and idly watching Poland's catastrophe. The Polish people had always found themselves in the middle of European political intrigues; they suffered most as a result. It is possible, therefore, to assume that the steamer that hits the German ship stands for Russia. Its crew, similar to that of the German vessel, does not care for the fate of the Poles trapped on the lower decks.

In other books and essays, Conrad's attitude toward Russia is more explicit. For the Polish-English writer, this country embodies evil; it represents to him what Nabokov called *poshlust*. The most straightforward references to Russia appear in Conrad's essay "Autocracy and War," where he writes: "There is an awe-inspiring idea of infinity conveying the word *Neant*—and in Russia there is no idea. She is not a *Neant*, she is and has been simply the negation of everything worth living for. She is not an empty void, she is a yawning chasm open between East and West; a bottomless abyss that has swallowed up every hope of mercy, every aspiration towards personal dignity, towards freedom, towards knowledge, every ennobling desire of the heart, every redeeming whisper of conscience."[29]

It is difficult to forget this biting tirade when one reads Conrad's only novel that deals straightforwardly with Russia, *Under Western Eyes*. Conrad often claimed that he was trying to be as objective as possible when writing this novel. Yet his prejudice toward and hatred of Russia, the country that deprived him both of his childhood and parents, can be felt throughout the work. In this novel, the writer returns to the themes of betrayal and exile, of which he never tires. Razumov, the main protagonist, feels guilty for betraying Victor Haldin, an anarchist who kills the Russian minister of interior. Razumov's remorse is no less intense than that of Lord Jim, who jumps off the *Patna* in time of danger. Both characters choose exile, yet their guilt follows them wherever they go. Conrad's obsession with this problem becomes the obsession of his fictional characters. He himself can never forget his own flight from Poland and his desertion of the country of his parents. Through the writing of *Under Western Eyes*, Conrad comes to terms with his own conscience, and yet the price of this reconciliation is his protagonist's death.

Razumov's exile in Switzerland is not much different from that of his counterparts. Yet, there is a significant difference in Conrad's treatment of the Russian character. Unlike Kurtz, who has never written a book and who almost willingly succumbs to the powers of darkness, the Russian exile has the privilege to complete one. Conrad offers Razumov writing as a means of survival: "Write. Must write! He! Write! A sudden light flashed upon him. To write was the very thing he had made up his mind to do that day."[30] Although Conrad suggests art as a means of survival in "Heart of Darkness," the intensity of Conrad's insistence on this idea in *Under Western Eyes* is of a different order altogether. By writing his diary, as Jeffrey Berman points out, Razumov is paving his way to "psychic relief from the agonizing guilt arising from his betrayal of Haldin."[31] I would add that Razumov is searching not only for "psychic relief" through his writing but also, most important, for transcendence of exile.

When Razumov appears close to resolving the problems of his exile he meets a barrier. Conrad makes Razumov encounter Miss Haldin, Victor's sister, who, like many other Conradian women, becomes the cause of the protagonist's tragedy. Miss Haldin is resolved to go back to Russia and work for the betterment of this autocratic society. Now, after the execution of her brother, she dwells even more than in the past on the terrible problems Russian society faces. Unfortunately for Razumov, he falls in love with the young woman; his diary and his writing no longer help him. He has to confess to Miss Haldin; she is the one who stands for Russia, and consequently, his past; only she can redeem his betrayal. His confession purges him, but, at the same time, it leaves him crippled for life.

Razumov returns to his past, to Russia, with no hope for salvation. Conrad sends him into the "bottomless abyss," although he knows that had he himself returned to Poland he probably would have shared Razumov's fate. But Conrad survives. He makes his narrator, an English gentleman, reset the imperfect diary into the accomplished form of the novel *Under Western Eyes*.

According to Jessie Conrad, the writer's wife, her husband's resolution of Razumov's fate exacted a high price.[32] After completion of the novel, Conrad suffered a severe breakdown that lasted several months. But Conrad was ready to pay even at the expense of his own health, for through writing he was fighting for survival during his long years of exile. His problems with transplantation were deep-seated. He could not spare the lives of his heroes, since they were forms of his alter ego that had to be subdued for the writer to be at peace with himself. Although the deaths of his doubles brought Conrad temporary relief, only continuous writing on his part could secure his own survival.

To commemorate his final victory of transcending exile through art, Conrad created still another novel, appropriately entitled *Victory*. Here again we see the recurrence of the idea that an exile who clings to the past and completely identifies with it brings upon himself his own death. Heyst, the protagonist of the novel, is from Sweden, a country geographically close to Poland. He settles first in London and then moves to the Pacific. Unlike Conrad's other characters, he does identify himself as an exile. He seems to understand what the essence of exile is. "'I am a transplanted being,'" he confesses to Lena, "'Transplanted! I ought to call myself uprooted—an unnatural state of existence; but man is supposed to stand anything.'"[33] Heyst's last sentence is ironic in view of the ending of the novel: he commits suicide.

When the Swedish transplant decides to make an island his permanent home, he thinks that doing so will ensure his survival. In Conrad's view, though, this self-imposed estrangement and isolation are not the proper means to transcend the "unnatural state of existence." Even though Heyst surrounds himself with familiar objects from his past (books written by his father, the old man's portrait, different household items), he nevertheless goes occasionally to the mainland. These visits become rarer as time passes, and so Heyst is now called by the people who know him "the Detached Heyst." Yet complete neutrality and detachment are impossible. Heyst may not go into the world, but the world will inevitably come to him. And come it does. On one occasion Heyst ventures off of his island and stays at a motel belonging to a despicable German. There he meets Alma, who is constantly being harassed by the owner of this establishment. Heyst takes a liking to the girl and helps her escape to the island. The two fall in love and resolve to lead a happy family life. Yet as we have already seen in Conrad's other works, the lovers' resolution contradicts the author's own intentions.

Alma becomes to Heyst what Miss Haldin became to Razumov. She is the past from which Heyst is trying to flee, although subconsciously he clings to it with all the passions of his transplanted nature. It is interesting to note that Heyst never calls Alma by the name with which she introduced herself to him; instead, he addresses her as Lena, a name popular in Slavic countries. It is he, thus, who calls the readers' attention to the fact that she represents the past. In the course of events, Lena dies in her efforts to save Heyst's life from unwelcome intruders. She views this sacrificial act as her personal victory over the powers of darkness and the beastly passions that govern the lives of many with whom she comes in touch: "Her eyelids fluttered. She looked drowsily about, serene, as if fatigued only by the exertions of her tremendous victory, capturing the very sting of death in the service of love."[34]

Conrad's descriptions of Lena betray the writer's deep admiration for her. She is ready to die for the man she loves, and Conrad appreciates her bravery. The victory, though, is not only Lena's. It belongs mainly to Conrad, who by sacrificing the two lovers secures his own existence. It is he who survives and transcends exile. Through his art, the Polish-English author learns how to resist the claims of the past and remain free from the temptation to become "one of them."

Two

VLADIMIR NABOKOV

The Russian Colossus in Exile

Mary

> *The best part of a writer's biography is not the record of his adventures but the story of his style.*
> Vladimir Nabokov, *Strong Opinions*

The story of Nabokov's style, which had its roots in Russia, was never constrained by geographical boundaries; it touched the minds and hearts of the foremost intellectuals in the Russian emigre circles of London, Berlin, and Paris and made its way across the ocean to America, where it is still being unraveled by literary historians and critics and constantly providing a few everlasting moments of pleasure to all those who come into contact with it. The story of Vladimir Nabokov's style is the history of building a shrine to art: the bricks are the writer's books, cemented together by his poetry, and the shrine's only inhabitant is beauty. *Mary* (published in Russian as *Mashenka*) was the first brick of this edifice; this novel was the starting point in Nabokov's stylistic development.

Mary was written in 1925 and published in 1926 by Slovo, a Berlin-based emigre publishing house. It did not go unnoticed by the critics, as Ludmila Foster in her article "Nabokov in Russian Emigre Criticism" points out,[1] but it did not receive the appraisal and attention it deserved. Nabokov was praised for his remarkable ability to convey the mood of frustration then prevailing among thousands of exiled Russians who were roaming helplessly over Europe with Berlin as their headquarters. They were trying to find new beginnings and to put down new roots in alien countries that were, nevertheless, close to their birthplace. At the same time, the writer was criticized for his failure to create a hero who aroused in readers a sense of tragedy. Most reviewers confined their task to a mere retelling of the plot of the novel, occasionally pointing out the psychological modalities of both the characters and the story itself; others tried to uncover parallels between Nabokov and his Russian predecessors.

The evaluations of American, British, and Australian critics of *Mary*, which became available in English translation only in 1970, did not vary greatly from those written by their Russian counterparts. Despite their advantage of being familiar with most of the writings of Nabokov, by then the well-established and renowned author of *Lolita*, critics only partially succeeded in providing a deeper insight into the workings of Nabokov's first novel.

The plot of *Mary* is simple and does not impose as strenuous demands upon the reader's imagination and intellectual abilities as Nabokov's later novels do. Lev Glebovich Ganin, a former soldier of the Russian White Army, a chess player and poetry lover, a physically and mentally sturdy young man, finds himself utterly bored with and weary of his three-month-old love affair with his simpleminded and pretentious mistress, Lyudmila Rubanski. In addition, he feels suffocated by the stifling and unbearably grim atmosphere of his boardinghouse, or *pension*, which shelters ghostlike and pitiful characters, all Russian emigrants. Among them is a poet, Anton Sergeyevich Podtyagin, who is dying from a heart ailment as well as from the loss of his ability to create poetry; Anton is trying in vain to obtain an exit visa to France. He is looked after by Klara, a 26-year-old "full-breasted girl,"[2] who is hopelessly in love with Ganin and fading away in an unidentified office where she works as a typist. Ganin's next-door neighbor is Alfyorov, a pseudomathematician and a most despicable creature; at present, Alfyorov is fully absorbed by his expectations of reunion with his wife whom he left behind in Russia after fleeing from the Red Army. He is ceaselessly made fun of by Kolin and Gornotsvetov, two homosexual Russian ballet dancers in search of engagements and artistic careers. "Presiding" over her tenants is the landlady, Lydia Nikolaevna Dorn, "the widow of a German businessman who twenty years ago brought her from Sarepta and who a year before had died of brain fever" (p. 5).

Numerous times, Ganin has forwarded notices of his forthcoming departure to Lydia Nikolaevna, but each time he was unable to tear himself away from this shelter of desperation and futile hopes. He does not know how to turn his desires into action, how to free himself from the web of passivity, apathy, and "perpetual waiting" in whose captivity he has been for the last several months. To free himself he would have to define his desires clearly and to know precisely what he wants:

> He was powerless because he had no desire and this tortured him because he was vainly seeking something to desire. He would not even make himself stretch out his hand to switch on the light. This simple transition from intention to action seemed an unimaginable miracle. (p. 18)

When the story opens, Ganin is living off his meager savings; but only two months previously, like so many other Russian exiles, he had been in constant pursuit of a job, any job. He was willing to work as a clerk or a waiter, or as an extra in a film shooting, as long as these occupations could satisfy his basic needs. Yet, none of these jobs was able to sustain the alert and searching mind of a well-educated young man who, unlike most of those around him, is able to distinguish good art from bad art, a fine poet from a mere scribbler. Intellectually Ganin perceives the absurdity and misery of his present situation, but in order to move out of the bewitched and vicious circle of his internal spiritual paralysis, something extraordinary, some "unimaginable miracle" coming from the outside world, as well as from within his own self, has to happen to him. Throughout the novel, Nabokov makes it clear that there is no easy way out of the dark labyrinth of forced exile with its winding paths and numerous dead ends. But he always provides hope of salvation lurking in the distant and temporarily uncertain future, some possibilty that a true Nabokovian character may find the right exit.

The opening scene of the novel takes place in an elevator, suspended in time and space (as are the two participants of this episode, Alfyorov and Ganin). Andrew Field, in his pioneering study *Nabokov: His Life in Art* (1967), errs when he asserts that the reader realizes only several chapters into the novel that the book's opening scene, the first encounter between Ganin and Alfyorov, takes place in an elevator.³ There are several keys, both in the Russian original and in the German translation of the novel, to the exact place of the opening scene.⁴ Although the wisdom of such a lengthy inquiry into what appears at first sight to be a minor and trivial mistake may be questioned, I will, in the course of my discussion, try to prove that Nabokov did not attempt to disguise the locale of the opening scene; on the contrary, he wished his reader to identify it immediately, since this knowledge is inseparable from one's understanding of this book.

In the stalled elevator, Alfyorov tries to strike up a conversation with Ganin, who is in no mood for idle talk with a man who cannot even pronounce his name correctly. The darkness that envelops the blacked-out cage of the elevator depresses Ganin; he is irritated by Alfyorov's treading on his foot; he is impatient to get out. Nervously shrugging off the suggestion made by the feebleminded Alfyorov that their unexpected meeting is symbolic, he sighs in deep relief when the lights come on, for he can finally make his way out of the elevator and into his room to ponder his miserable existence.

The elevator is the first in a chain of several cagelike images created by Nabokov in this novel. The parent-cage is exile from which there is rarely escape, but which, as becomes clear later in this novel as well as in Nabokov's later works, can be transcended by the human mind, by intellect, and, finally but most important, by art. The movie theater to which Ganin takes Klara and Lyudmila one evening is another cage where illusions are perceived as real life. The boardinghouse is also a cage, holding its seven shadowlike inhabitants, placed there by capricious fate whose workings only God and the writer know.

Putting Ganin into each of these cages, Nabokov makes him

go through a thorny and exasperating journey toward self-realization and self-esteem. One of the most revealing episodes in the novel has Ganin viewing a film in which he performed as an extra, a demeaning occupation reluctantly accepted by many of his compatriots as one of the few available means of making some money.[5] The tragedy of these "heedless extras," to use Ganin's expression, stemmed from the fact that they "knew nothing of the picture in which they were taking part" (p. 22). Life was bypassing them in a cruel and hideous manner. Ganin is ashamed to recognize himself among the extras of the film. He sees himself, or his doppelganger, clapping to the order of the director of the film, a "fat, red-haired, coatless man" who is "yelling himself to insanity through the megaphone" (p. 21). He feels embarrassment not only for himself but for all the emigrants, "those innocent exiles, old men and plain girls who were banished far to the rear simply to fill in the background" (p. 21). One man especially attracts his attention:

> Ganin's doppelganger also stood and clapped over there, alongside the very striking-looking man with the black beard and the ribbon across his chest. Because of that beard and his starched shirt he had always landed in the front row; in intervals he munched a sandwich and then, after the take, would put on a wretched old coat over his evening dress and return home to a distant part of Berlin, where he worked as a compositor in a printing plant. (p. 21)

In this passage, Nabokov expresses the essence of the drama of exile as well as hints at the probable ways of intellectual survival, which presupposes, as one of its most important elements, the preservation of one's true identity. It is interesting to notice, in the opening of this paragraph, how Nabokov shifts from the description of Ganin's doppelganger to the description of another character—the "very striking-looking man"—who departs from the story as casually as he enters it, but whose appearance, if only for a fleeting moment, makes a deep and unforgettable impression and leaves a lasting trace both upon the mind of the reader and upon the texture of the book.[6] The two layers of clothes that the "striking-looking man" is wearing serve as a metaphor for not only the situation of this particular person, who is just another face in the crowd, but that of an entire stratum of displaced people. Under the "wretched old coat" of the present there is an "evening dress" and a "starched shirt"—relics of the past, worn now to add credibility to a game put on by those who do not care for the real man who is hidden under the innocuous frame of a secondhand coat. The misery of this particular exile is heightened when the reader finds out that he is forced to live in a distant part of Berlin and to take an unpretentious job as a compositor in a printing plant. The occupation with which Nabokov endows the man is important—as a typesetter he is close to the written word. Whenever any of Nabokov's characters have a direct or even indirect connection with the written word, with literature, or with art in general, the reader can be sure that there is a chance for intellectual survival and that the shabby coat may someday be exchanged for one that will unite appearance with reality.

The film and the "haggard image" of himself on the screen release a flood of emotions that threatens to envelop Ganin but that he successfully withstands. Trying to understand what is happening both to him and to other exiles, his conclusion is simple, but its importance is difficult to overstate: "We do not know what we do" (p. 22). As soon as he is able to perceive this fact, he finds the direction toward self-recognition—he is on his way toward discovering what to do and how to do it.

Coming to terms with one's present situation and understanding the essence of one's existence are not enough to cure oneself of the disease of exile, the symptoms of which are inertness, impotence, and moral and intellectual stagnation. There is still a burden one has to free oneself of—the burden of the past, the burden whose weight and gravity make their carrier bend and look downward. And Nabokov does not abandon Ganin when the latter is halfway toward giving up his shadowlike existence; he comes to his help and offers a cure, which becomes the remedy for complete recovery for many of his artist figures.

Insomnia is a typical affliction of a Nabokovian character, and Ganin is no exception. After seeing Lyudmila home from the movie theater, he spends a few wakeful hours in his room, during which he starts to see clearly the futility of the dead-end liaison with his mistress, whose constant prattle about dresses, hairdressers, and other trivia makes him nervous. His thinking is interrupted by Alfyorov's monotonous humming in the adjacent room. Ganin cannot stand it any longer; he pulls on his trousers and thumps on the door of his neighbor, whose company he has been trying to avoid since their first encounter in the elevator. Alfyorov jumps at the opportunity to have a visitor with whom he might discuss his wife's arrival from Russia on Saturday. It is Alfyorov, however, who does all the talking, which centers on his wife Mary and Russia, while Ganin works on a solution of a chess problem that he found drawn on a piece of paper on his host's bed. Suddenly he is attracted by a word uttered by Alfyorov—the word *accursed* is used by Alfyorov to describe Russia. The following short conversation takes place:

"What did you call Russia?"
"Accursed. It's true, isn't it?"
"I don't know—the epithet struck me as curious." (p. 24)

In this passage Ganin first displays his interest in words as well as shows his interest in chess, and it is well known that Nabokov has a near obsession with both chess and words. But Ganin shares more than intellectual interests with Nabokov; their deep affinity is revealed by a biographical similarity, as Nabokov himself discloses in the twelfth chapter of his memoir, *Speak, Memory*, when he recalls his first love, Tamara, whom he met when he was fifteen years old and whose loss he finds analogous to the loss of his motherland: "for several years, until the writing of a novel relieved me of that fertile emotion, the loss of my country was equated for me with the loss of my love."[7]

The novel Nabokov has in mind is *Mary*. But if the writing of a novel helped its creator overcome the tragic sense of loss, what is there that Nabokov's double must overcome to assuage his sense of loss? Ganin is not writing a book—not yet—but he has memories, which are indispensible for creating one someday. During the four days prior to his departure from the *pension*, starting with that wakeful night, he recollects the events of his past associated with *his* love, Mary, who by cruel coincidence—

an ever-present phenomenon in Nabokov's writings—happens to be Alfyorov's wife. She arrives on the day that Ganin decides to leave. It was during his visit to Alfyorov, the proprietor of the golden beard, which (in a typical Nabokovian metamorphosis) changes from golden to yellow, and, finally, to dung-color by the end of the novel, that Ganin found out Alfyorov's relationship to Mary. She was Ganin's first genuine love; he was at that time still reverently carrying around her letters in his wallet. Ganin is shocked to see the pictures of Mary, no longer *his* Mary, shown to him by her now even more despicable husband.

The life of the novel, like Ganin's own life, then takes a new turn. The curative process does not start immediately; Nabokov is still not sure whether the reader fully comprehends that state of utter dejection in which Ganin lives. Chapter 3 of the novel, though only two pages long, is a powerful account of the essence of loneliness, alienation, frustration, and desperation. This brief vignette, charged with inexplicable beauty and horror that often only poetry can convey, dramatizes the state of an alien soul lost in the darkness of an alien city in which the timing of the cold and bleak neon lights can be planned in advance, whereas human thought takes its own heed and direction. This state of absolute depression can be enlivened, at least partially, by memory, a particular memory, for example, that of "a woman's face, resurgent after many years of humdrum oblivion" (p. 27). But this momentary, though so sweet, indulgence in the bliss of past happiness may in its turn be interrupted by the quite ordinary voice of a casual passerby, inquiring about the closest grocery store or any other prosaic or trivial matter, which brings the "rememberer" down to earth again, making him recognize that he cannot sustain himself by feeding on the past only. This is not to say that memory as a tool to resurrect the past should be entirely abandoned; rather, it is to suggest that not everything that happened in the past is of equal importance. Memory, therefore, should be selective, choosing only the most significant moments to bridge the gap between past and present.

The beginning of Ganin's recollections of his first love coincides, curiously enough, with his first energetic and meaningful step toward action. Once his memories of Mary start to engulf his whole being, he finds it rather easy to break off his meaningless relationship with Lyudmila Rubanski. There are no more obstacles to prevent him from resurrecting his past life, in comparison with which the reality of the present looks bleak and illusory—indeed, not real at all. Despite this, Ganin does not lose touch with his environment; conscious of both time and space, he manages to keep both planes of his existence in balance:

> Time for him had become the progress of recollection, which unfolded gradually. And although his affair with Mary in those far off days had lasted not just three days, not for a week but for much longer, he did not feel any discrepancy between actual time and that other time in which he relived the past, since his memory did not take account of every moment and skipped over the blank unmemorable stretches, only illuminating those connected with Mary. Thus no discrepancy existed between the course of life past and life present. (p. 55)

Letting the readers penetrate Ganin's mind and follow the workings of his memory, Nabokov reveals the full strength of his protagonist's artistic character. "Memory," Nabokov has said, "is really in itself a tool, one of the many tools an artist uses."[8] This tool is inseparable from creative imagination, which in itself is, according to Nabokov, a "form of memory."[9] Ganin is able to combine the two, thus making his recollections assume a life of their own.

Ganin's recollections of his past love are both sketchy and detailed. He can glance over a year in his relationship with Mary but dwell for a long time on memories of his parental garden, or on a pavilion where he met Mary, or on a birch tree. He laments the fact that "memory can restore to life everything except smells, although nothing revives the past so completely as a smell that was once associated with it" (p. 60). But the lost smells of the past can be rehashed by the smell of carbide [coming from the trains, passing by the *pension*], that "brought back everything at once" (p. 67). Past and present are inseparable, a continuation of the same process; to understand the present, Ganin has to understand the past and see their interdependence.

His deep absorption in his memories, however, does not make

Ganin blind or insensible to what is happening around him. He finds time to help the dying poet, Podtyagin, to overcome the bureaucratic prerogatives of the pedantic German officialdom (Ganin speaks good German) and to obtain an exit visa to France. He tries, though in vain, to dispel Klara's suspicion that he is a thief, a suspicion she conceived when she found him rummaging through Alfyorov's drawers in search of Mary's photograph. He takes an active part in the farewell party thrown by Gornotsvetov and Kolin. He visits his landlady, who liked him more than any of her other tenants, in order to take his leave. All this is done while Ganin is on his way toward achieving a definite resolution of his life. The final touches to this resolution are added when he approaches the end of his reminiscence about Mary, about his past, about his Russia. The Russia that on the first day of recollections was the only thing that he would call real (Berlin and its inhabitants being unreal and illusory) becomes by the end of the fourth day "What it was in reality; the distant past" (p. 113). Recognizing this, Ganin can look at the world with new eyes, and "this fact meant a secret turning point for him, an awakening" (p. 113).

A blind attachment to the past, the inability to transcend former experiences, the failure to notice that the barren months of winter are followed by the blooming of lilac in spring can only lead to death. Anton Sergeyevich Podtyagin, the poet who was once known and loved in Russia and whose lines Mary quotes in her letters, dies at the end of the novel; Ganin goes on living. Their visions and dreams of Russia differ drastically. Podtyagin, when he dreams of his motherland, is always left wth sensations of terror, pity, and disgust. He tells Ganin: "It's terrible—oh, terrible—that whenever we dream about Russia we never dream of it as beautiful, as we know it was in reality, but as something monstrous—the sort of dreams where the sky is falling in and you feel the world's coming to an end" (p. 81). There is no salvation for the old and ailing poet who lives in the darkness of his past. Despite the deep sympathy Nabokov feels for him (he even endows him with the first name of Chekhov and with the patronymic of Pushkin, for whom he had deep respect and love), Anton Sergeyevich Podtyagin has to die, which he does after losing his passport with the exit visa to France in it.

Podtyagin's grim vision of Russia is countered by that of Ganin who, in reply to the poet's dream, says that he "only dreams about the beautiful things. The same woods, the same country house. Sometimes it's all rather deserted, with unfamiliar clearings. But that does not matter. We have to get out of here, Anton Sergeyevich" (p. 81).

"Here" is where the poet perishes; "here" is where Alfyorov, with his Leninesque beard, the true representative of *poshlust*— "the obviously trashy, the falsely important, the falsely clever, the falsely attractive"[10]—will disappear in his trivial, easily adaptive, rootless, and mundane existence; "here" is where, for the first time, Ganin is able to see that the loss of Russia is not necessarily the end of one's desire to live.

When at the beginning of the novel Ganin sets out to recreate a world that is no more, he feels as if he were a god; by the end, there is no way to tell the difference between Ganin the god, who recreates a world he once knew, and Ganin the artist, who places into this world the story of his lost love, the story of Mary. By reliving his past, Ganin relieves himself of the "fertile emotion" associated with the loss of his country, equated by him with the loss of his love. So did Nabokov when he wrote his first novel. This is, then, what Nabokov has to offer to Ganin; this, and something more. The last pages of the book become a plea to Ganin, a plea expressed by Mary in one of her letters: "Write, write for God's sake, write often and more" (p. 90).

On the morning of Mary's arrival, after taking a cold and refreshing shower, Ganin makes his way to the train station. He intends to meet Mary, whom he has decided to take away from Alfyorov. With two suitcases in his hands, he casts a last glance toward the boardinghouse "where he had been reliving his past and to which he would never return again" (p. 113). He is not sorry to leave this haven of pitiful shadows. For a moment, flashes of the past sweep through his mind, but they are swiftly replaced by a vision of the present. Behind the public garden near the train station, Ganin spots another house that is now in the process of being built:

> The wooden frame shone like gold in the sun, while on it two workmen were passing tiles to a third man. They lay on their backs, one above the other in a straight line as if on a staircase. The lower man passed the red slab, like a

large book, over his head; the man in the middle took the tile and with the same movement, leaning right back and stretching out his arms, passed it on up to the workman above. This lazy regular process had a curiously calming effect; the yellow sheen of fresh timber was more alive than the most lifelike dream of the past. As Ganin looked up at the skeletal roof in the ethereal sky he realized with merciless clarity that his affair with Mary was ended forever. It had lasted no more than four days—four days which were perhaps the happiest days of his life. But now he had exhausted his memories, was sated by them, and the image of Mary, together with that of the old dying poet, now remained in the house of ghosts, which itself was already a memory.

Other than that image no Mary existed, nor could exist. (p. 114)

The symbolic significance of this passage is difficult to overstate; it is the key to understanding both Nabokov's first novel and those written later. The half-built house, situated next to a garden in full bloom, is constructed of slabs associated by Ganin with books. This house is analogous to the edifice that Nabokov constructs throughout his long and fruitful literary career for the sake and in honor of the vital and life-giving powers of art. This elaborate structure has its roots in both past and present; it can be built only if its builder is industrious and patient, only if he constantly keeps up his hard but rewarding labor, only if he looks upward instead of downward.

Neither Mary, who bears the taint of *poshlust*, Alfyorov's legacy to her, nor the old dying poet is among the future inhabitants of this house. An overpowering, disabling, and paralyzing memory has no place there. The artist who suffers from terrifying dreams, who is unable to transcend man-made boundaries constricting his art, who cannot make his poetic voice heard through fate's inexplicable and sometimes cruel ways, has no place in Nabokov's edifice.

The juxtaposition of the two houses that Ganin observes prior to his departure to new and nameless regions where visas aren't required—art does not need a visa—inserts a heightened note of optimism and belief in survival through art and intellect in distant, and often alien environments. One has confidence in Ganin, the artist whose imagination is finally realized in actions. Therefore, one can only partially agree with Professor Lee's conclusion that "the essence . . . of the novel is loss—loss created by the constant interweaving of past time and present time" and that Ganin's "real life lies in his past which is both recoverable and lost."[11] The loss of one's birthplace is, indeed, a painful and tragic experience, but the point of Nabokov's book is that the sense of evanescence can be overcome by will. Ganin may for the rest of his life remain a *Hotelmensch*, to use George Steiner's term for Nabokov, but as a true artist like Conrad's Marlow or Singer's Jacob, he will overcome any formidable obstacles placed in his way by the caprices of life. Nothing could stop Marlow from keeping his boat intact and proceeding toward the deep and terrifying darkness of the Congo; nothing could prevent Jacob from carving the Ten Commandments on the unyielding and harsh surface of a rock, found in an alien land, in order to create a symbol of freedom and survival.

Ganin is finally free from and out of the suffocating cages of his former prosaic existence; however, he is yet to appear, time and again, in various countries and under different disguises, in the writer's later books. He will go wherever Nabokov takes his double.

THE REAL LIFE OF SEBASTIAN KNIGHT

> *My private tragedy, which cannot, indeed should not, be anybody's concern, is that I had to abandon my natural language, my natural idiom, my rich, infinitely rich and docile Russian tongue, for a second rate brand of English.*
> Vladimir Nabokov, *Strong Opinions*

[handwritten marginalia: but l / Lolita]

Thirteen years and eight books separate *Mary*, Nabokov's first novel written in Russian, from *The Real Life of Sebastian Knight*, his first work created in English. The difference in languages does not obscure the striking similarities and affinities, both thematic and structural, between the two books. There is no doubt, however, that Nabokov's tenth novel, though written in a language other than his native tongue, bears the mark of a more mature and skillful artist, aware not only of what he wants but also of how to bring his art to near perfection. Nabokov's first English novel reflects the significance of his shift from Russian to English prose, which cannot be understood without at least a brief explanation of what happened to Nabokov, the citizen, and Nabokov, the writer, during his thirteen years of exile in Berlin.

Political and social events, in both Russia and Europe, during the turbulent and dramatic years preceding the Second World War, brought an end to the sacred dream that was reverently cherished by many exiled Russian writers—the dream of a return to their motherland. The irony of their situation was underscored when the 1936 Nobel Prize was awarded to Bunin, a prominent Russian exiled author. This tribute of honor and acknowledgment became, at the same time, the death seal to a generation of men of letters who were the proud carriers of the rich tradition of Russian literature, but whose rootlessness and displacement brought upon them the curse of sterility. Authors like Bunin, Remizov, Adamovich, Gippius are now disavowed and scorned by the "free" and "happy" Soviet critics; if any of them is occasionally mentioned, he is referred to as an *enfant terrible*, duly punished for his refusal to accept the rigid and soulless dogmas of a party-controlled existence.

The endurance and intellectual survival of the above-mentioned writers for nearly two decades of postrevolutionary exile must even now be viewed as a miracle, made possible only by art and strong will. The existence of Russian journals, magazines, and publishing houses in Europe brought a measure of stability to their situation. The majority of them never thought of writing in a language other than their own. However, the atmosphere of assurance and artistic security that the Russian publications provided began to give way to feelings of hopelessness and pessimism with the advance of Nazism in Germany. As a result, the center of the Russian intellectual milieu shifted from Berlin to Paris. The French capital became for most of the exiled artists the last destination, from which there was no exit but to oblivion.

Nabokov clearly saw the situation developing around him. There was no reason for the writer and his family to stay in Berlin; Vera Nabokov, née Slonim, was Jewish; her husband himself was resistant to any prejudice and to anti-Semitism in particular. He fought it whenever and wherever he was able to do so; his outspokenness on this topic made even some of his best friends feel uneasy, and they warned Vladimir that he might bring trouble upon his family unless he kept silent. But instead of being quiet and sharing the fate of the many Jews and non-Jews who became victims of their inability and unwillingness to see clearly the prewar reality, which was already contaminated by Nazi slogans, pogroms, and concentration camps, Nabokov moved his wife and his only son to Paris in 1937. That the writer had no illusions about what was to become of Europe in just a few years is shown in *The Real Life of Sebastian Knight*, which contains a masterfully realized scene of a funeral in a Jewish home in 1936 that foreshadows the Nazi atrocities as well as the tragic destiny of a whole people. The narrator's foresight and sagacity proved to be prophetic indeed.

It was in France, his new country of exile, that Nabokov wrote his first English novel. Writing in a new language was not an easy endeavor, to be sure. True, he had been educated in Cambridge, England, and he had learned English from governesses in his parents' home, but one can only guess how much agony the writer had to endure when, in order to survive as an artist, he gave up his "infinitely rich and docile Russian."[12] Prior to writing *The Real Life of Sebastian Knight*, Nabokov had only one literary venture in English. In 1936 he translated his novel *Despair*, which was published in 1937 by the English firm John Long. Later in his life, Nabokov time and again recalled his switch from Russian to English prose as something "exceedingly painful—like learning anew to handle things after losing seven or eight fingers in an explosion."[13]

According to Nabokov's own testimony, he knew in 1936, when he was working on the translation of *Despair*, that he "would eventually land in America" and "use English as a wistful standby for Russian."[14] To come to such a conclusion, for somebody who held his native tongue in such great esteem and used it not just as a means of communication but as a medium of artistic expression, meant, to a large extent, the beginning of a completely new life in an utterly different linguistic atmosphere. Part of the writer's artistic identity had to be left behind, and his first nine Russian novels have come to be seen as first chapters of a book to be completed in the future. It was easy for Nabokov, forty years later, to assert that he relieved himself of the burden of the past after writing his first novel, *Mary*. Yet, this statement is only partially true. Nabokov's continuous creation of fictitious characters who may consciously perceive that past times are by-gone but who still cling to them with the stubbornness of a nursing baby whose mother's breast is dry testifies to the author's inner struggle between the dictates of necessity and the idealizations of the past.

A good illustration of this point is the story "The Doorbell," included by Nabokov in his book *The Return of Chorb*, published in 1929. It is representative of the problem in question insofar as it deals with exiles who are unable to understand that there is no return to the past. When they finally recognize this truth, it leaves them with a bitter taste in their mouths and a mirthless smile on their faces.

Nikolay Stepanovich, the protagonist of the story, decides after seven years of roaming all over the world to go to Berlin and visit his mother whom he has not seen since he left Russia. He is full of expectations of a happy reunion, full of energy and conviction that this reunion will bring an end to his wanderings and become a turning point in his life. By coincidence, he finds his mother's address easily and sets out immediately for her apartment. The woman who opens the door only barely resembles the image he has been cherishing during long years of separation. She is made up to look young; the evening dress she has on, as well as the table set for two, testify to the fact that she is expecting a visitor. But she is not expecting her son. The twenty-five candles stuck in a birthday cake betray the age of the guest about to arrive. Bewildered, embarrassed, and hesitant, torn between the temptation to open the door when her young friend arrives to celebrate his birthday and her motherly instinct to hold back her son when he decides to leave, she wants to explain, to make things clear; but no explanation will suffice, since her son by now understands the real state of affairs. He departs as suddenly as he had entered, leaving his mother on the divan sobbing tears that destroy the carefully applied makeup and reveal the true face of an old and tired woman—a pitiful character indeed. The meaning and the irony of the situation are not difficult to grasp; there is no return, new beginnings cannot be found in the past. By trying to recover his past and have it take the place of the present, an exile, Nabokov implies, is committing a destructive error. The most a transplant can hope to achieve is at least a tentative reconciliation between his past and his present, rather than having one exclude or take precedence over the other.

Nine years later, while living in Paris, Nabokov expresses the same idea, though in a more subtle and straightforward manner, in his short Russian poem "We So Firmly Believed." The poet looks back at his past and is astonished to see "to what a degree you, my youth, / seem in tints not mine, in traits not real."[15] Though it is obvious that one cannot forget and lightheartedly dismiss long years of exile, an admission of this kind does not come easily. But the voice in the poem recognizes that only radical actions can make the poet sound fresh and new again. This is not to say that the past has to be blocked out completely; rather, it should be seen as an "outline—the / hero of any first chapter"(p. 89). The agony and the triumph of this conclusion are beautifully rendered in the last lines of the poem:

You've ceased to be I . . .
      . . . yet how long we believed
that there was no break from the damp
      dell
to the alpine heath.

(p. 89)

This poem can justifiably stand as an epigraph to *The Real Life of Sebastian Knight*, on which Nabokov was working at the time he wrote it. But the novel goes beyond the poem: it is not only a farewell tribute to his past; it also marks the beginning of a new and fruitful literary career for Vladimir Nabokov.

V., the narrator of Nabokov's first English novel, decides to write the authoritative biography of his half brother, Sebastian

Knight, six years his junior, who died in March 1936. V. knows that it is not going to be an easy task to write about his novelist-brother with whom he had only a few brief meetings. During his inquiries into Sebastian's personal and professional lives, which V. starts almost immediately after Sebastian's death, he finds out that Mr. Goodman, his brother's former secretary, has already completed a book on his deceased employer, entitled *The Tragedy of Sebastian Knight*. V.'s meeting with Mr. Goodman as well as his reading of the book of this miserable scribbler make him even more convinced that there is a need for another work on his artist-relative. Mr. Goodman's Grub Street production fails entirely to portray the real life of Sebastian Knight and reveals that he has probably not read any of Sebastian's novels in their entirety.

V. makes up his mind to adhere to two principles. The first is to be faithful to facts and facts only, to dismiss anything that might be insignificant and superfluous. This stand echoes Nabokov's own views regarding biography as a genre; the writer's demand upon his future biographer is indeed high: "I would ask my biographer—plain facts, no symbol searching, no jumping at attractive, but preposterous conclusions, no Marxist bunkum, no Freudian rot."[16] The second principle, which will enable V. to write the real biography of Sebastian Knight, has to do with the latter's literary legacy. The narrator accuses Mr. Goodman of never quoting anything from Sebastian's five books to support his seemingly insightful speculations. He, for his part, will use his brother's novels as often as possible, citing long or short passages whose content and significance will exclude mere conjecture or falsification. This same principle was faithfully employed by Nabokov himself when he wrote his tribute to Gogol.

Like any writer of a biography, V. correctly assumes that he should talk with and seek information from people who personally knew Sebastian or those who were in close touch with him. Most of them, though, do not prove helpful; they saw only Sebastian's surface, misunderstanding the real character of Sebastian Knight.

The beauty and meaning of *The Real Life of Sebastian Knight* cannot be grasped by reading the novel once. As Nabokov himself instructed his readers, "You can only re-read a novel. Or re-

[margin note: cf. Brian Boyd's biographies of N.]

re-read a novel."[17] And indeed, after the first reading of this
novel, one will certainly be attracted by the writer as conjurer,
as enchanter, as shaman. To be sure, Nabokov's tricks, twists in
the plot of the story, allusions to chess, and striking coincidences
do awe the reader, who is delighted by the fine mind of the com-
poser and left to wonder at the skillfullness of a writer who has
the story of V.'s search and the account of Sebastian's life so artistically juxtaposed. But behind all this the "real" book can be
easily lost.

After at least a second reading of this book, much that does
not seem of great importance at first sight assumes significance.
The crucial point to recognize is that it is not just a biography
that V. is writing but rather the autobiography that his half
brother Sebastian would have written, as he had indeed planned,
had he not died prematurely. This leaves one to ponder the real
relationship between V. and Sebastian Knight. The novel is not
long, however, and the last page of the book yields an easy solution to this query, a solution that, on second thought, has been
foreshadowed from the beginning of the work. V. and Sebastian
are one and the same person.

V. acknowledges his inseparability from Sebastian when he
comes to the end of his brother's story: "'Thus—I am Sebastian Knight,'" [18] he says. This statement echoes the narrator's
thoughts when he is only contemplating writing the biography
and is offering reasons for his decision to do so. He is, according
to his own admission, the only man who has the "inner knowledge" of Sebastian:

> Inner knowledge? Yes, this was a thing I possessed, I felt it
> in every nerve. And the more I pondered on it, the more I
> perceived that I had yet another tool in my hand: when I
> imagined actions of his which I heard of only after his
> death, I knew for certain that in such or such a case I
> should have acted just as he had. (pp. 33–34)

To make his point even stronger, V. introduces the following illustration: he compares himself and Sebastian to two tennis
players whose strokes might have been totally different, but the
"general rhythm of their motions as they swept all over the

court was exactly the same, so that had it been possible to draft both systems two identical designs would have appeared" (p. 34). Commenting on Sebastian's novels, V. remarks that he knows them "as well as if I have written them myself" (p. 203). Endless parallels of this kind can be cited.

The device of the double or the psychological notion of the split identity is, in the case of this novel, a convenient tool, explored by the author to its fullest. Time and again, V. implies that no one but himself has the "inner knowledge" of Sebastian Knight and, therefore, that he is the only person who is able to give a faithful, truthful, and precise account of his character. In addition, tracing numerous biographical similarities between Nabokov and Sebastian Knight—date of birth, education, interests, writing, chess—one can confidently affirm that the author generously endows the fictitious writer with features and characteristics of his own that he usually imparts only to those of his heroes with whom he feels close affinity. This becomes even more significant when we keep in mind that *The Real Life of Sebastian Knight* is the first book written in English by this Russian writer. Thus, Nabokov also is writing an autobiography, one that deals with a period in his life that can be termed the European exile.

But if there is such a closeness between the author and Sebastian, why does Nabokov make the latter die? Why is it that Sebastian has to share the fate of another writer, Anton Sergeyevich Podtyagin in *Mary*? Why, even though he is a fine artist, does Sebastian perish? What is the sin for which he has to be so cruelly punished? The answers to these crucial questions can be found if we take a close look at the development of the plot and the interplay of themes in this novel.

Describing Sebastian's methods of writing (they bear a striking resemblance to Nabokov's), V. comments that Sebastian "had always liked juggling themes, making them clash or blending them cunningly, making *them* express the hidden meaning, which could only be expressed in a succession of waves, as the music of a Chinese buoy can be made to sound only by undulations" (p. 176). There is a need, therefore, to read Nabokov's writings according to the author's own suggestions; the "absolute solution" to the questions posed by the reader is "there,

[handwritten marginal note:] Sebastian K. = N's European autobiography; but can this be assumed only because N. and V. share certain characteristics?

somewhere, concealed in some passage" one reads too hastily or it is "intertwined with other words whose familiar guise" (p. 180) may often deceive even a careful observer.

V., like Ganin in *Mary*, employs the technique of writing from memory, a tool that is indeed indispensable to the creation of art. Time and again, he explains that memory is selective and fragmented, retaining only the most significant details of the past, though such details may seem trifling and unimportant to a casual onlooker. The demand upon the reader's imagination is high—he should, in order to enjoy and perceive the work of the writer, be able to make connections and establish associations among the flashes of memory that resurrect different events. The reader must become actively involved in the creation of a novel, or, in this case, the recreation of an artistic career of a writer of five books. Sebastian's image does not appear to V. as part of his boyhood, "thus subject to endless selection and development, nor does it appear as a succession of familiar visions," but it comes "in a few bright patches, as if he were some erratic visitor passing across some lighted room and then for a long interval fading into the night" (p. 18). The night, that is, the darkness of one's being, has to be penetrated and conquered to yield sufficient information about the man behind the books.

Sebastian's mother, an Englishwoman by birth, left the family when he was only five years old. His father married again, this time to the woman who was to become V.'s mother. This marriage, too, lasted only briefly; Mr. Knight was killed in a duel, trying to defend the honor of his first wife who was living a frivolous life, traveling constantly from one capital of Europe to another, from one spa to the next. Only once did she come to visit her abandoned son and then just for a few moments. This encounter, as becomes clear later in the novel, has a strong and lasting impact on the boy. V., while searching in Sebastian's drawers after his death, finds in one of them a "small muslin bag of violet sweets" (p. 17)—a present given to Sebastian during his fateful rendezvous and guarded reverently for many years. She was a strange and unpredictable woman, the kind that did not hesitate to make a fuss in a hotel if a maid did not live up to her expectations. Although V. confines himself to a rather sketchy portrayal of Sebastian's mother, he nevertheless finds it neces-

like Rushdie

sary to point out that "Sebastian could never forget his mother, nor could he forget that his father died for her" (p. 18).

Sebastian started to write while he was still a teenager. His poems were in English, invariably signed with a "black chess-knight drawn in ink" (p. 17). Everything that surrounded him encouraged his literary pursuits: he "was brought up in an atmosphere of intellectual refinement blending the spiritual grace of a Russian household with the very best treasures of European cultures" (pp. 15–16), a description that fits well with Nabokov's childhood surroundings and upbringing.

Sebastian's family, like those of many other Russian exiles, was forced to leave the mother country, fleeing a regime described later by Sebastian in most unflattering terms. He could never rid himself of the loss he suffered, nor was he able to avoid themes relating to his motherland. In his fifth, and last, novel, *Doubtful Asphodel*, he vented his anger at suppressors of individual freedom in the harshest terms he could find. In the same novel Sebastian attacked totalitarianism in general, and Russia in particular; he called the latter "a dark country, a hellish place" to which there was no return at any cost. " 'If there is anything of which I am certain in life,' " he wrote, " 'it is that I shall never exchange the liberty of my exile for the vile parody of home' " (p. 26). Yet, in another novel, *Lost Property*, Sebastian dealt with the emotions experienced by those who had to leave their country, calling the purest of the emotions those of a "banished man pining away after the land of his birth" (p. 26).

Unlike the rest of his family, Sebastian, instead of going to Paris, went to study in Cambridge, where despite all the efforts he made to "out-England England" (p. 46), he could never "fit into any kind of picture" (p. 44). He was, according to V. as well as those who came in close touch with him, a man "blissfully condemned to the solitary confinement of his own life" (p. 46).

V., true to his principles of biography, takes a very close look at Sebastian's literary legacy. He provides the reader with a brief but detailed synopsis of his brother's first novel, *Prismatic Bezel*, which, like Nabokov's *Mary*, goes almost unnoticed by the critics. The second novel, *Success*, enjoys a higher degree of acknowledgment and is promptly followed by a compilation of three stories, of which "The Back of the Moon" is the most noteworthy. Although tired and fatally ill, Sebastian nevertheless finds enough creative powers in himself to write yet two more books—the autobiographical novel, aptly entitled *Lost Property*, and his most grim but beautifully written book, *Doubtful Asphodel*. Each of these works is heavily quoted by V.; when commenting upon them he does not fail, in order to make a point, to supplement his remarks by references to Sebastian's letters to his editors, as well as to the latter's scarce personal correspondence. All of Sebastian's novels to some extent resemble in theme and structure the novels that Nabokov wrote in Russian in the late 1920s and 1930s. Although this similarity has been noticed by many students of Nabokov, one point needs to be stressed. It appears that Nabokov, by writing his first English novel, was summarizing his own career as a Russian writer, practicing, with the help of his invented narrator, the well-established mode known as autocriticism.

While analyzing, interpreting, and explaining Sebastian's novels in order to achieve a sense of objectivity in his judgments, V. faithfully reproduces opinions and explications expressed by other critics. In some cases he agrees with them, but more often than not he refutes their critiques. His heaviest fire is directed against Goodman. Critics of this kind, according to V., should not only be forbidden to touch upon a subject that deals with writers of Sebastian's caliber; they should be forbidden to write at all. V. ridicules criticism that sees a human being in absolute dependence on society and under the unconditional dominance of his environment, without ever giving a thought to what this human being can do in order to shape the course of his own life. (Nabokov would certainly share V.'s sentiments: the content of Goodman's "treatise" and the dishonest methods he used in writing it can appeal only to "mediocrities," to use one of Nabokov's favorite terms.) V., as one might expect, saves his most biting satire and hilarious raillery for the discussion of the book's language, which consists mostly of weather-beaten clichés and ready-made phrases that this Grub Street hack uses to express trivial and shallow ideas. He even tried to change an epithet in one of Sebastian's books, thus committing the unforgivable sin.

The same high standards that Sebastian applies to other writers and critics he also applies to his own writing. He experi-

Nabokov an autocritic in Sebastian Knight

ments with different modes and methods of composition, but it is with the excellence of the written word and the perfection of style that he is primarily obsessed. "His struggle with words," V. writes, "was unusually painful and this for two reasons. One was the common one with writers of this type: the bridging of the abyss lying between expression and thought" (pp. 83–84). The second had to do with the fact that Sebastian "had no use for ready-made phrases because the things he wanted to say were of an exceptional build and he knew moreover that no real idea can be said to exist without the words made to measure" (p. 84). Interestingly, V. hastens to remark that, although Sebastian's English thrived wonderfully, his Russian was "purer and richer than his English ever was, no matter what beauty of expression he attained in his books" (p. 85). V. finds it necessary to inform the reader that he is also taking his studies of English seriously in order to be able to write Sebastian's biography. It is he, rather than professional critics, who exhibits a genuine appreciation for the written word and the beauty it can convey, if utilized in a proper and orginal way.

All that Mr. Goodman perceived correctly was the fact that Sebastian's life was a tragic one, but this explanation of the tragedy was specious. Sebastian emerges both from his own books and from the information V. gathers from those close to him—a poet, a painter, a former schoolmate—as a major artist whose ways are not always easy to comprehend. Clare Bishop, the woman who could have been most helpful to V.'s search for his brother's true life, refuses to talk about the past and her relationship with her former lover. She knows more about him than anybody else, and it is not by chance that she is endowed with most of the characteristics and features that only a true Nabokovian woman can possess. Clare Bishop possesses a rare imagination, her sense of beauty is highly developed, her humor is of the most subtle artistic quality. In short, she is an artist in her own way— the only suitable kind of companion to a writer of Sebastian's caliber. And yet, Sebastian abandoned her, condemning Clare to a brief and unhappy existence with a man she had never loved. She dies in childbirth.

In one of Sebastian's books, there appears a letter in which a young man tries to explain to his mistress why he broke up their relationship. He says that he still believes he is in love with her but that there is another woman whose powers he is unable to withstand. Accidentally, the letter is found among many other objects in the wreckage of a crashed plane; the young man might have been among the perished passengers. This incident foreshadows Sebastian's death.

A thorough analysis of the novel yields a peculiar observation regarding the plots of Sebastian's novels and the story of V.'s search for the true identity of his brother; they seem to mirror each other. Thus the woman who lures the young man away from his mistress appears to have a counterpart in Sebastian's own life. According to his brother's will, V. has to burn two batches of letters that he finds in Sebastian's drawers. One set of letters is written in English and obviously belongs to Clare Bishop; the letters in the second lot are in Russian—their writer's name is not known to V., although he is aware of the existence of a Russian woman in the novelist's life who accelerated his death. Since V. burns the letters without even trying so much as to peep at their content, he has to rely totally upon himself in finding the femme fatale.

V.'s search starts with a hotel in France where Sebastian stayed when his break with Clare became common knowledge among their friends. Failing to procure the list of Russian women who stayed in the hotel at the same time, again by wonderful coincidence, V. comes across a peculiar gentleman named Mr. Silberman, who strikingly resembles a character, one of the best ever created by Sebastian, in his story "The Back of the Moon." It is Mr. Silberman who helps V. obtain the names of the women.

There are four addresses and four leads that V. has to pursue. Two women prove to be the wrong ones. The third is Helen Grinstein, a Jewish woman from Russia. Upon meeting her, V. immediately understands that she cannot be the one he is trying to locate, since "girls of her type," he says, "do not smash a man's life—they build it" (p. 37). His search finally brings him to the fourth woman, Madame Lecerf, who at first makes him believe that she is the best friend and confidante of Sebastian's former mistress. She tries to engage V. in a love affair and avoids telling him that she knows of the liaison between his brother and her friend. At their last meeting in Paris, she finally succumbs to V.'s insistence on being told all she knows and presents him with an unpleasant picture of Sebastian—the lover who becomes a nuisance, and, as a result of this, is thrown out of his mistress's house.

V. energetically rejects this vision of Sebastian; but despite the aversion that Madame Lecerf begins to provoke in him, he still visits her in a decayed mansion in the country, where a meeting between him and Sebastian's mistress is supposedly being set up by Madame Lecerf. Here in the country V. at last realizes that he has been made a fool of by Madame Lecerf and that she is the Russian woman, Nina Rechnoy, whom he was so eager to meet. He is astonished to find out that his brother could fall prey to a woman of her kind, who in more ways than one resembles Sebastian's own mother. Nina Rechnoy, alias Madame Lecerf, runs away from her husband and child like Sebastian's mother. Both lead a frivolous and hectic life; both have a destructive touch—whatever gets in their way withers and fades.

This woman then, so unlike Clare Bishop and Helen Grinstein, destroys Sebastian Knight; she, the mother, the mistress, the personified past all in one, curbs and drains the writer's creative powers. Here, then, are the answers to the questions posed earlier; Sebastian dies because he loses touch with reality; because he pursues a dream that can never come true; because he tries to recover an unrecoverable past. Ironically, Sebastian, the author of five English books, is known at the hospital where he dies as the Russian gentleman; his last letter, which starts out as a missive to Nina Rechnoy and turns abruptly into a farewell message to his brother, is written in Russian. Sebastian dies as a Russian, not as the Englishman he so wanted to be.

Sebastian's fate is a forewarning to V.—if the latter wants to become a true artist, he should not repeat Sebastian's tragic mistake. This is the admonition given to V. by Mr. Silberman, the self-appointed detective, in one of the most illuminating episodes in the novel—one that can justifiably be seen as the key to understanding the real life of Sebastian Knight.

On two occasions V. conducts peculiar short conversations with Mr. Silberman. The first time the following exchange takes place:

"You are a traveller?"
" I said yes."

"In what?" he asked, cocking his head.
"Oh, in the past I suppose," I replied. (p. 127)

And a few minutes later, when he is entrusted by V. to find the name of the Russian lady, he gives the narrator advice that could just as well have been addressed to Sebastian Knight and that, if accepted, might have prolonged his life:

"Forget her," he said. "Fling her out of your head. It is dangerous and ewsyless." (p. 128)

During their second meeting, Mr. Silberman reiterates his suggestion, this time in stronger and more emotional terms:

"I fink it is ewsyless. You can't see the odder side of de moon. Please donnt search de woman. What is past is past. She donnt remember your brodder." (p. 132)

V. accepts the old man's advice; he is able to withstand the temptations of Nina's powerful, destructive sexuality; he has won and his triumph is rewarded by the results of his painstaking search. He completes the task he had conceived several months previously; words, sentences, and paragraphs cover the pages of the notebook presented to him by Mr. Silberman, and they convey the true life of Sebastian Knight. V.'s book as well as Nabokov's novel is written in English.

V. Nabokov had written his first English novel, and one of the best American critics, Edmund Wilson, told the author that "it is absolutely enchanting. It's amazing that you should write such fine English prose and not sound like any other English writer, but be able to do your own kind of thing so subtly and completely."[19] Although Edmund Wilson later became angry at Nabokov (the two writers could never reach a mutual understanding concerning Russian prosody and the Soviet socialist system), Wilson never stopped being amazed at Nabokov's work.

PNIN

> *I shall continue to exist. I may assume other*
> *disguises, other forms, but I shall try to exist. I*
> *may turn up yet on another campus, as an old,*
> *happy, healthy, heterosexual Russian, a writer*
> *in exile, sans fame, sans audience, sans*
> *anything but his art.*
> Kinbote in *Pale Fire* by Vladimir Nabokov

One of the main reasons for the tragic fates of Alexander Sergeyevich Podtyagin and Sebastian Knight is their inability to balance the experiences of their past with the dictates of the present. Unless such an equilibrium is achieved, tragedy is predictable. To survive, Nabokov's characters have to learn how to walk properly along the tightrope of existence. Leading his heroes through their apprenticeship in the art of survival, Nabokov himself learns the necessary qualifications to sustain his own state of stability so indispensable to artistic creativity.

In 1942, in Wellesley, Massachusetts, where he was teaching at the time, Nabokov wrote a poem that reflects this dilemma and also characterizes his future writings in America. The poem, composed in Russian and then very skillfully translated into English by the author, is entitled "Fame." Such a poem, loosely termed a dialogue between soul and body, is often written by poets at a crucial point in their literary careers.

The fantasylike, surrealistic beginning of the poem immediately introduces the reader into the grim and tense atmosphere that dominates its first part:

> And now there rolls in, as on casters, a character,
> waxlike, lean-loined, with red nostrils soot-stuffed,
> and I sit and cannot decide: is it human
> or nothing special—just garrulous dust?[20]

Simultaneously, an unavoidable confrontation is set up between the "I" of the poem and what appears to be his alter ego who emerges as a most despicable creature, endowed with both human and nonhuman traits. It parades in front of its dumbfounded beholder under different disguises, hiding behind various masks, revealing thus its chameleon character. One moment it is a hangman, another minute it turns into an "evil old schoolmate" (p. 103). These vicious and haunting images torture the "meek heart" of the now speechless and fameless "I," the poet himself. Any attempt of the poet to raise his voice and do away with the undesirable visitor fails, drowned in the torrent of words this "garrulous dust" ceaselessly showers upon him. The only refuge left to the poet is his ability to think his own thoughts while his "visitor speaks—and weightily, folks,/and so cheerfully" (p. 105) utters pronouncements conducive to anything but cheerfulness.

The voice's statements all concern the poet's literary career, and are indeed harsh and cruel, not of the usual kind that the "I" is accustomed to hear time and again from his countrymen. Had he been accused of "changing countries like counterfeit money,/ hurrying on and afraid to look back" (p. 105), he could have had an immediate answer to these idle and slanderous charges:

> But my work, curved to form an aerial viaduct,
> spans the world, and across in a strobe effect spin
> of spokes I keep endlessly passing incognito
> into the flame-licked night of my native lands.
>
> (p. 105)

But the vicious creature's words go beyond this—they touch upon the most painful and tender parts of the wound it had itself inflicted upon the poet by the mere fact of its appearance to him. It says the writer's books will never be read by his countrymen although the books are written in a language they understand:

> "Your poor books," he breezily said, "will finish
> by hopelessly fading in exile.
> . . . your unfortunate books
> without soil, without path, without ditch, without
> threshhold
> will be shed in a void. . . .
>
> (p. 107)

What can be more painful to a writer than to see how his books—his children—become orphans even before their parent's death? Had they at least been read, and even condemned by the reader, their tragedy would have been less pathetic. To be deprived of an audience can mean only oblivion and, frequently, intellectual death, for both the artist and his literary efforts.

The despicable and nightmarish creature knows the agonizing thoughts of the exiled artist; it knows where the hurt is greatest—and directs its arrows there:

> "Who, some autumn night, *who*, tell us please in the backwoods
> of Russia, by lamplight, in his overcoat,
> amidst cigarette gills, miscellaneous sawdust,
> and other illumed indiscernibles—who
>
> on the table a sample of *your* prose will open,
> absorbed, will read *you* to the noise of the rain,
> to the noise of the birch tree that rushed up windowward
> and to its own level raises the book?"

(p. 107)

At this point in the poem, the writer manages to shake off the paralyzing effects of the biting tirade; he succeeds in inserting an aside by defining the theme and the main idea of the poem he is writing. He points out that the poem "Fame" is about the author's thoughts "of contracting the reader's awareness" (p. 109). By using this artfully realized insertion, the poet, the "wizard" as he calls himself, dispels the destructive charms of the evil spirit that only moments before had threatened his very existence. Furthermore, by addressing the reader directly, the poet succeeds in his efforts to "contract the reader's awareness" as well as in his quest to regain the peace of mind denied him by the unwelcome intruder. Now the intruder's vain and pointless promises of the materialistic paradise the poet could have enjoyed in his native country sound hollow and full of *poshlust*. He has more than this; he possesses something that nobody can take away from him, something that no money can buy or replace.

The mood of the second part of the poem is antithetical to that of the first. The reader cannot help laughing with the poet and sharing his happiness that "Conscience,/the pimp of my sleepy reflections and projects,/did not get at the crucial secret" (p. 111). But this secret is never straightforwardly stated by the poet. He does not want to be "overexplicit"; he relies on the reader, who in many ways should be the poet's reflection of his own self, to perceive the value of the precious gift of which he is the sole owner.

In the process of reading this poem, it becomes clear that the secret stands for art. The author possesses a rare tool that grants him the knowledge "how the self to transcend" (p. 111). It is the genius to create that enables Nabokov to build a viaduct, a bridge made of words, that brings the writer and the audience closer to each other and obliterates the distance between East and West. The tensions existing between the past and the present give rise to creative power. "This is why," he writes, "I find it laughable the empty dream about readers, and body and glory" (p. 111).

The bravado of this pronouncement should not be taken at face value. What would then be the use of writing this poem, of turning one's soul inside out? An audience is important to all writers, and Nabokov is no exception. The fact that he has created such a poem testifies to the drama of an inner struggle in the mind of the author. No doubt, the loss of Russia and the loss of an audience who can appreciate his "docile" and "rich" Russian is painful to the writer, even though he is trying to laugh away his anguish.

Time and again Nabokov addresses himself to the problem of audience as well as to the effects that the banishment of his books in Russia have on him. The explanations with which he supplies the reader are often as contradictory as the thoughts that preoccupy his mind during the confrontation of the "I" and its alter ego in "Fame."

Twenty years after completing this poem, Nabokov said in one of his interviews, "I don't think that an artist should bother about his audience. His best audience is the person he sees in the shaving mirror every morning. I think that an audience the writer imagines, when he imagines that kind of thing, is a room filled with people wearing his own mask."[21] The paradox inherent in this statement is obvious: on the one hand, he plays down the role of an audience, yet, on the other, he provides a detailed description of the reader he would like to have, namely, a reader who has close affinities with the writer himself.

In 1937, when Nabokov decided to write his first English novel, he already knew that creating in English meant a clear-cut break from Russian. This is not to say that this resolution would not bother him in the years to follow. In 1964, in an interview with Alvin Toffler, he tried to explain why he had abandoned for good his native language, and again the problem of audience is dealt with paradoxically. Nabokov reiterates his intention to write in order to "please one reader alone—one's own self." But he hastens to remark that "one also needs some reverberation, if not response, and a moderate multiplication of one's self throughout a country or countries; and if there be nothing but a void around one's desk, one would expect it to be at least a sonorous void, and not circumscribed by the walls of a padded cell."[22] Hence, the writer's decision to create in English is made to obtain a new audience. One has, of course, to be just to Nabokov and see beyond the utilitarian aspect of this resolution. Writing in English may, eventually, have some "reverberations," but, in addition, the shift from one medium of expression to the other provides the artist, according to his own admission, with a totally new experience—the "excitement of verbal adventure."[23] And what an adventure it turned out to be!

Nabokov laments the poverty and rigidity of *his* English too often for any intelligent reader to believe in the truthfulness and sincerity of this self-criticism. Like many exiles who manage to master a foreign language and are frequently fishing for compliments by underplaying this achievement, Nabokov is not above affectation. He, like any other mortal, needs encouragement, praise, and refutation of his half-joking and half-serious self-accusations. "My English," he says, "this second instrument I have always had, is however a stiffish, artificial thing, which may be all right for describing a sunset or an insect, but which cannot conceal the poverty of syntax and paucity of domestic diction when I need the shortest road between warehouse and shops. An old Rolls Royce is not always preferable to a plain Jeep."[24] (Well, I'll do what he wants me to do: "Oh, no, no, Mr.

Nabokov! Your English is beautiful, it is superb. . . . I just wonder, how come you have never learned to drive a car, be it a Jeep or a Rolls Royce?")

Thus, as becomes clear from my reading of the poem "Fame" as well as from the discussion of the importance of an audience to a banished artist, Nabokov's past experiences and present preoccupations with the quality of his language will always be in the background of his literary endeavors. They will not, however, be able to take the upper hand and cripple his artistic creativity. Sometimes the burdens of the past may outweigh the light, insecure acquisitions of the present. The confrontation between the two is unavoidable and sustains the friction, the tension that sparks the artist's inspiration.

In his earlier books, Nabokov, though fond of his central characters, has invariably sentenced them to death, thus assuring his own survival. When he gained new powers and his art started to acquire new dimensions and depths, there was no longer any need to have his main characters die. Pnin, the protagonist of his American novel of the same name, is spared the destiny of Podtyagin and Sebastian Knight. He transcends his exile and survives; although he is often treated in a harsh manner by the omniscient narrator, Pnin is nevertheless granted the green light when he chooses to leave the story. It is true, though, that Pnin's departure happens only after he has drained the cup filled with the sour broth of the exiled artist's experience.

Nabokov was more fortunate than many other exiled intellectuals who fled Europe to escape Nazism and destruction. He immediately found a friend, Edmund Wilson, who took great interest in both the personal and professional life of the Russian writer. Stalinism and pro-Stalin feelings were very widespread in America in the 1940s. There was little likelihood that an anti-Soviet Russian author would be warmly embraced by the literary circles in the United States. Although Wilson was also overcome by the euphoria over the so-called achievements in the USSR (fortunately he got over it when the purges of Stalin in the thirties became common knowledge among even the always doubtful American intellectuals), Wilson was the first critic to recognize the literary merits of Vladimir Nabokov. His remarks about the Russian writer's books were always helpful and encouraging. As early as 1941, Wilson called Nabokov a "first-rate poet" and added that *The Real Life of Sebastian Knight* "has stimulated me more than any new book I've read since I don't know what."[25]

Not always did Wilson like what Nabokov wrote in his novels. His harsh criticism of *Lolita* was offensive and unjustifiable. But when he liked something, he said so without sparing words of praise. Upon the publication of *Pnin* in its entirety, Wilson expressed his sincere appreciation and approval of the novel: "I think it is very good, and also that you may at last have made contact with the great American public."[26] This was a flattering yet true statement from one of the foremost literary personalities in the United States. On the other hand, though, the critic's pronouncement conveys an inherent paradox: the Russian-American author is finally going to make "contact" with his new audience through a novel that is, after all, about the constant failures of an exiled intellectual to establish this "contact" with his new country as well as with his new countrymen.

Nabokov started to work on *Pnin* prior to his publication of *Lolita*. The first four chapters of the novel appeared in the *New Yorker* as separate stories over the period from 1953 to 1957, and only in 1957 was the novel published in its entirety. The serial publication of the book prompted some critics to consider it not as an integral whole but, rather, as a compilation of short stories held together in a somewhat artificial manner. Howard Nemerov regards *Pnin* as an "accidental" novel and doubts its integrity.[27] Yet another critic perceives that it is "marvelously realized throughout, but fails to progress" and then proceeds to argue, too elaborately, that *Pnin* has been structured by Nabokov in the fashion of a Cinderella fairy-tale.[28] However, a careful reading makes it clear that the book progresses and that all of its seven chapters are tightly structured and obviously under firm control. Quite frequently, as we have seen, Nabokov's statements contain contradictions and inconsistencies. But when he himself says that "the design of *Pnin* was complete in my mind when I composed the first chapter,"[29] we can only accept this utterance at face value. Furthermore, familiarity with Nabokov's working habits removes any doubts as to the integrity of the novel.

The omnipresence of the narrator signals the strict unity of

every part of the novel. In the last chapter of the book, he sheds
all disguises and appears in flesh and blood, in order, I believe,
to dispel any confusion that might have arisen in the reader's
mind as to the true nature of both the story and the storyteller.
He does not loosen his control over his characters even for one
moment. The narrator is always there to comment and to help
us to understand how important this story is if one wants to
comprehend fully the nature of exile and the destiny of a banished artist. Pnin's survival in alien, often unfamiliar and hostile
surroundings is also the narrator's survival. The latter never
fails to guard Pnin from the pitfalls and temptations that the
new society has to offer. To become "one of them," he indirectly
suggests, is to lose identity, is to melt into the new environment,
with the result being intellectual death.

The narrator's most crucial comment comes in the first chapter, and it coincides with his first tangible appearance in the
novel. What he has to say at this point is central to the understanding of the novel and should be considered the governing
principle of both Pnin's and his own future fate:

> I do not know if it has been noted before that one of the
> main characteristics of life is discreteness. Unless a film of
> flesh envelops us, we die. Man exists only in so far as he is
> separated from his surroundings. The cranium is a space-
> traveler's helmet. Stay inside or you perish. Death is di-
> vestment, death is communion. It may be wonderful to
> mix with the landscape, but to do so is the end of the
> tender ego.[30]

Later conflicts arise from the exile's desire to achieve communion, to divest himself of that part of his identity that remains a
mystery to those who surround him, and, on the other hand,
from the strong will to preserve one's "tender ego." In short, in
order to survive a transplanted intellectual must learn how to
balance the past and present and make the two nourish rather
than destroy each other. To perceive clearly how such an equilibrium can be achieved and what techniques the author employed to do so, we must look closely at the main character.

[handwritten margin note: necessary to maintain original identity]

[handwritten note at bottom: Prof. Pnin: an example of the past-present balance necessary for the exiled intellectual]

For the reader to understand the nature of Pnin, he must be taken seriously. As alive as any character in fiction can be, Pnin is flesh and blood and shares many affinities with Nabokov. Pnin's true identity can be missed entirely if one considers him a clown in the literal meaning of the word, as one critic does when he says, "it should be our . . . task to examine just how the author succeeds in creating a clown whom the reader is prepared to take seriously."[31] The struggle of a displaced person, banished from his own culture and language and confronted by a new, often hostile environment, may indeed seen funny to some readers who are satisfied to see the novel's surface without ever taking the trouble to explore its depths. They judge Pnin from their own standards and preconceived notions, failing to recognize a very simple fact—to understand a character means at least partially to identify with him. Only a few characters in Nabokov's *Pnin* are capable of understanding the protagonist; to the rest he is a "freak," who is there for their own amusement.

The reader's first encounter with Pnin comes when he is told that Pnin is on his way to Cremona to deliver a lecture entitled "Are All the Russians Communists?" Timofey Pnin is worried about the manuscript (he is anxious not to mix it up with two other papers he wants to read on the train), about his passport, about money. Of his additional trouble—being on the wrong train going in the wrong direction— he is not yet aware. Despite all the complications that result as a consequence of this situation, he still makes it safely to Cremona and presents his lecture. But one opening episode requires further explication.

Sitting hunched up on a park bench, pondering his confusion with the timetables, Pnin suddenly feels a sensation that he has already experienced on several other occasions: he feels as if he is having a heart seizure. Pnin's thoughts about his supposed heart ailment, which has not been uniformly diagnosed by his various doctors, turn gradually to his past life and pre-exile experiences. It is at this point and for the first time in the novel that Nabokov skillfully applies the technique of shifting from present to past and then again to present. The execution of this technique is much more subtle in this book than in Nabokov's previous novels. This is due to the narrator's constant intrusions into the story, while Pnin is deeply absorbed in the reveries of his past, in order to comment on the protagonist's thoughts, background, and whatever else might be relevant to the reader's understanding of him. Not until he is done with his asides, remarks, commentaries, does the narrator allow Pnin to shake off his sometimes painful reminiscences and return to the present. This technique of shifting between present and past, supplemented by the narrator's comments, becomes a recurring pattern.

Thus, when Pnin is still on his journey into his childhood during this first near heart attack (two more to follow later), the narrator tells the reader about Pnin's life in Russia, his parents, his education. When he feels that he has provided the reader with sufficient information, he withdraws and lets the reader directly penetrate Timofey's own mind. Pnin recalls an episode that occurred during a critical childhood illness. The most vivid image that his mind has preserved from those early childhood days is that of the wallpaper whose pattern always left him puzzled:

> He has always been able to see that in the vertical plane a combination made by three different clusters of purple flowers and seven different oak leaves was repeated a number of times with soothing exactitude; but now he was bothered by the undismissable fact that he could not find what system of inclusion and circumscription governed the horizontal recurrence of the pattern; that such a recurrence existed was proved by his being able to pick up here and there . . . the reappearance of this or that element of the series, but when he tried traveling right or left from any chosen set of three inflorescences and seven leaves, he forthwith lost himself in a meaningless tangle of rhododendron and oak. (p. 23)

Pnin, as we see, does not have too much trouble understanding the "vertical plane" of the pattern; what troubles him most is the "horizontal recurrence" of the combination and it is the latter he wants to decipher, since he feels that the understanding of it will regain for him "his everyday health, his everyday world;

and this lucid . . . thought forced him to persevere in the struggle" (p. 23).

A rereading of *Pnin* reveals the writer's intention of drawing such an elaborate pattern, consisting of vertical and horizontal planes, which, as becomes clear, stand for Pnin's past and Pnin's present, respectively. Timofey Pnin cannot comprehend one without considering the other; past and present are inseparable; whenever Pnin tries to grasp the meaning of his present existence or come to terms with it, he invariably ends up taking a journey into his past. The mere repetition of this demanding and tiresome exercise will, he hopes, teach him how to walk the tightrope of existence.

When Pnin finally comes out of his swoon, he sees in front of him "a gray squirrel sitting on comfortable haunches" (p. 24). This little rodent will time and again cross the winding paths of Pnin's story, always accompanying Pnin's memories of the most crucial events of his past. It becomes a signal placed on the crossing of the vertical and horizontal planes, helping the reader to recognize the turn when Pnin is taking the vertical plane. Later in the novel, the writer explains the meaning of the word *squirrel*—it originates, he says, "from a Greek word which meant 'shadow-tail'" (p. 87). On a different occasion, we find a peculiar occurrence of the word *shadow*, but in another context. As I have mentioned earlier, Pnin suffers from a heart ailment; when the doctors examined him they were always baffled, vainly trying to "puzzle out what they termed 'a shadow behind the heart.'" It is clear that the metaphorical meaning of shadow is the shadow of the past constantly trailing Pnin's present existence. Pnin needs to learn not how to rid himself of it but how to live with it.

Within a matter of hours, during the lengthy and senseless introduction of Pnin to his Cremona audience, he experiences another seizure, similar to the first. And again Pnin's thoughts turn to the past. The public is metamorphosed into a vision of ghosts among whom Pnin recognizes his parents, his deceased friend Vanya Bednyashkin, his aunts, his former sweetheart Mira Belochkin (*belochka* in Russian means *squirrel*)—all of them "murdered, forgotten, unrevenged, incorrupt, immortal" (p. 27). It is incomprehensible to Pnin, even after so many years in exile, why only bloodshed, cruelty, and massacres could change the history of a country that had been his motherland. With thirty years' hindsight, he sees clearly that the Russian Revolution has done nothing for the people it promised to liberate; on the contrary, it has brought destruction and built a new form of tyranny. (Nabokov's first novel written in America, *Bend Sinister*, is entirely devoted to this theme.) But the twentieth century, Pnin seems to imply, was not satisfied with the destructive course of the October Revolution. It still had to produce a Hitler and a Holocaust that resulted again in the senseless murder of millions upon millions of innocent people. The torturing thoughts of this atrocious event in mankind's history come to Pnin during still another heart seizure, this time at the estate of Al Cook, an exiled Russian himself, who every other year gives a reunion party for his countrymen in America.

Such a reunion inevitably resurrects past events in the lives of its participants. Pnin, for his part, is reminded of his former sweetheart, Mira Belochkin, the daughter of Dr. Belochkin, who was Pnin's father's personal friend as well as the family doctor. Mira was Jewish and she shared the fate of many other Jews at Buchenwald, which, as Pnin points out, was only an "hour's stroll from Weimar, where walked Goethe, Herder, Schiller, Weiland, the inimitable Kotzebue and others" (p. 134). To understand how so monstrous an event could have happened in a civilized society is beyond Pnin's imagination. One probably has to "kill . . . common sense," [32] as a character in Aharon Appelfeld's story "Badenheim 1939" suggests, in order to make at least some sense of what was going on. This pronouncement echoes the opening statement of a course taught at Waindell College by Pnin's colleague, best friend, and landlord, Laurence Clements, according to which "the evolution of sense is, in a sense, the evolution of nonsense" (p. 32). Pnin tries to find some respite from these dreadful memories in his attempts to forget the unforgettable:

> In order to exist rationally, Pnin had taught himself, during the last years never to remember Mira Belochkin . . . because, if one were quite sincere with oneself, no conscience, and hence no consciousness, could be expected to subsist in a world where such things as Mira's death were

possible. One had to forget—because one could not live
with the thought that this graceful, fragile, tender young
woman with those eyes, that smile, those gardens and
snows in the background, had been brought in a cattle car
to an extermination camp and killed by an injection of
phenol into the heart, into the gentle heart one had heard
beating under one's lips in the dusk of the past. (pp.
133–34)

It is not difficult to identify with Pnin's desire to forget, to blot
out the grim memories of a life marked and influenced by the
most sordid events of the century. But the desire to forget and
the inability to do so go hand in hand. Just as Nabokov could not
bury the needless bloodshed in 1917 he could not obliterate the
memories of the "Nansen-Passport period," that is, his European
exile, a time marked by his notable literary achievement but
also marred by the advance of Nazism and all that accompanied
it. The bitter thoughts of his brother's death in a German concentration camp never abandoned the writer.

How could then Nabokov create a "freak" in the person of
Pnin, a man who in many ways shares the writer's own most
tragic experiences? The author himself supplies an answer to
this question by creating a cohort of clowns led by the main
jester and buffoon in the court of the Waindell campus pseudo-
scholarly community, Professor Cockerel. To these people Pnin
seems clownish; but he is never perceived as such by Nabokov's
sympathetic characters, Victor, Joan, Laurence among them.

Although considered insane and freakish by the outside world,
Pnin refuses to surrender himself passively to the circumstances
imposed upon him by exile. He acts, he creates, he speaks; in
short, he is alive. Regardless of his tragic understanding of the
"history of the world as the history of pain" (p. 167), Pnin still
sets his task—indeed, his quixotic mission—to change the world,
while he himself is also ready to undergo certain changes. According to Pnin, "it was the world who was absent-minded and
it was Pnin whose business it was to set it straight" (p. 13).

To reward Pnin for the loss of his former love, the author creates Victor, the son of Liza and her German husband Eric Wind.
Victor, as Douglas Fowler points out, is a Nabokov "favorite."[33] It

is in him that Pnin finds some consolation for his confusing and often burdensome life on Waindell campus. The boy emerges as a true artist in search of his own artistic identity and creative powers. In Pnin he finds the spiritual father for whom he longs; Pnin, in turn, wholeheartedly accepts the young man and is ready to do for him anything that he would have done for his own son, had the past not prevented him from having one. When questioned about the influence of Joyce's writings on his own literary production, Nabokov was always ambiguous in his responses. Despite his reluctance to respond directly, it is difficult to overlook the parallel that exists between the relationship of Pnin and Victor and that that of Bloom and Stephen Dedalus in *Ulysses.*[34]

It is Pnin's and the narrator's victory as well, that despite the burdens of the past, Pnin still seems to manage in the present, enriched now by the existence of Victor, and does not fall prey to a love that never materialized, to a dream that would inevitably have had tragic consequences. Even while Pnin "would remove his glasses to beam at the past" and indulge in those "unforgettable digressions of his," which invariably concerned bygone times or his scholarship, he never failed to massag[e] the lenses of the present" (pp. 10–11). Nabokov is always on the alert to balance the two elements of his protagonist's life.

Pnin at times seems funny, but he is never clownish. He acts as a *zerstreute Professor* (p. 13) when he places a call for a book that he has already checked out from the library; his "flirting" with different gadgets may call for laughter; his constant complaints about the "sonic" noises in the houses he occupies may provoke ridicule. But these are human traits that should be understood, not labeled as "freakish." Isn't it the insensitivity of his new countrymen that causes their unfavorable response to Pnin? Nabokov surely thinks so. One has only to juxtapose the two parties, Russian and American, to come to a similar conclusion.

At the first, on the estate of Al Cook, the host is Nabokov's example of what results can be achieved by one's divestment of his past, one's communion with the surroundings. Al Cook's Russian name was Kukolnikov, but it has been blatantly Americanized. The alteration of the name leads to other changes too. Nobody would be able to tell Al Cook, the business executive, the Mason, the golfer, who speaks a "beautifully correct, *neutral* English" [my emphasis] (p. 115) from any other American. And, yet, there is something more to this man, something that neither exile nor circumstances could mute and maim. Somewhere deep in his soul he remains Russian, and only when "some very old and beloved Russian friend was his midnight guest would Alexander Petrovich suddenly start to discuss God, Lermontov, Liberty, and divulge a hereditary streak of rash idealism that would have greatly confused a Marxist eavesdropper" (p. 115). Alas, as Nabokov lets his reader understand, such things happen to Alexander Petrovich only at midnight and very rarely. He has become "one of them" and is as neutral and colorless as his English.

Yet it is his "hereditary idealism" that makes Al Cook gather at his home his Russian friends—writers, scholars, poets, and artists—who managed to make it to America but who cannot and will not forget their homeland. Their conversations take place on a high intellectual level. Their interests range from philosophy to literature, from history to painting. They indulge in the intellectual feast of their reunion with the same enthusiasm they exhibit toward hearty Russian dining. Rarely is there any backbiting or gossip here; respect and honor for each other govern their conduct.

In one of the conversations there is an allusion to Sirin, an emigré Russian writer who frequented Al's parties on earlier occasions. Another former guest who is mentioned, though absent now, is Vladimir Vladimirovich, a famous lepidopterist. It is not difficult to put two and two together: Sirin was Nabokov's pen name in his Russian novels; Vladimir Vladimirovich is his first name and patronymic. That Nabokov is a lepidopterist is well known. Sirin is not only an occasionally mentioned name among the guests; he is also, as we find out later in the novel, the renowned Anglo-Russian writer who comes to replace Pnin in Waindell College. In addition, he is the narrator of *Pnin*, who appears in the seventh chapter in the book. This technique of making a physical appearance in his own novels had already been used by Nabokov in his earlier works, particularly in his Russian novel *Laughter in the Dark*. The reason for doing this is not the writer's desire to commemorate his own self but, rather, to exhibit the very tight and dictatorial control he has over his characters and material. In addition to the dramatic action of the novel, the use of such authorial devices testifies to the unity of Nabokov's works in general and in *Pnin* in particular.

While teaching Russian on Waindell campus, Pnin has been simultaneously working on a very ambitious study entitled *Petite Histoire* of Russian culture, "in which a choice of Russian curiosities, Customs, Literary Anecdotes, and so forth would be presented in such a way as to reflect in miniature *la Grande Histoire*—Major Concatenations of Events" (p. 76). Even in his scholastic and artistic endeavors Pnin remains a "traveler in the past" (p. 76), but, contrary to Podtyagin and Sebastian Knight, he does not ignore what is going on around him. To celebrate the completion of his study as well as the end of the academic year, Pnin decides to give a party for several of his colleagues and acquaintances. With the exception of Joan and Laurence, the party is attended by people who have nothing in common with the host. According to the latter's own admission, the party had "body but it lacked bouquet" (p. 145). Conversations are mostly centered around campus gossip and the bowl of punch. The more drunk the guests get, the more freely they express their ignorance and naiveté. The only sober views are those held by Joan and her husband, who in many ways resembles Pnin: "the two men . . . were really at home only in their warm world of natural scholarship" (p. 40). The rest of the guests are characterized by people like Hagen, the head of the German department, whose sole criticism of the Nazis concerned their tasteless choice for the location of Buchenwald—too close to the birthplace of Goethe. Another cartoonlike character at the party is the English professor. He hardly opens his mouth; he is too deeply absorbed in contemplating his memoir, which he thinks will be an immensely valuable asset to posterity. Again, as at the Russian party, the Anglo-Russian writer is mentioned. Only Joan, the true Nabokovian character who shares many similarities with Clare Bishop, is allowed to speak of him and discuss his methods of composition. Her remark can easily refer to Nabokov: "'But don't you think—haw—that what he is trying to do—haw—practically in all of his novels is—haw—to express the fantastic recurrence of certain situations?'" (p. 158). Joan is also the only woman who understands Pnin; more than that, she genuinely loves him and is ready to come to his help when he needs her. People might call each other by their first names at this party but there is not a trace of friendship or mutual respect among them. (Russians, as Pnin points out, use the first name and patronymic to address one another; formal as it may sound, there is more feeling in it for a Russian than any first-name calling might convey.)

The party has more significance for Pnin than appears at first. Its timing coincides with his decision to settle down and buy the house in which he resides. He has never before owned a house and is quite tired of having to move so frequently. Joan remarks that "if anybody needs a house, it is certainly Timofey" (p. 165). The thought of finally settling down and having a nook of his own "was to Pnin something singularly delightful and amazingly satisfying to a weary old want of his innermost self, battered and stunned by thirty-five years of homelessness" (p. 143). But Pnin's desires come into conflict with those of the author. Always on the move, restless and changing places, known as a reliable tenant to his colleagues who rented their houses to him when on leave, Nabokov himself never bought a house to live in permanently. This is not to say that he did not long for a quiet abode of his own, but to be always on the move seems to be in the nature of an exiled artist, who often does not plant firm roots in one place. (The same was true for Joseph Conrad as well as for his characters.) Nabokov provides us with yet an additional reason for such mobility: "nothing short of a replica of my childhood surrounding would satisfy me."[35] To settle permanently would mean to share the fate of Al Cook, to become "neutral," to divest oneself of one's own identity.

To prevent Pnin from becoming "one of them" Nabokov has him fired, or "shot" in Pnin's broken English. It is not accidental that the bad news is being conveyed to Pnin by Dr. Hagen, the novel's most hated character, the only person, Nabokov implies, capable of "quench[ing] a messy cigar in an uneaten bunchlet of grapes" (p. 170). The author has no intention to soften the "punishment" he inflicts on Pnin for his desire to blend with the landscape. Pnin's bitterness at the way life is treating him is underscored by yet another discovery—he is to be replaced by an Anglo-Russian writer who according to Nabokov's complicated design is not only the narrator and the author of the novel in which Pnin is the protagonist, but who also happens to be his former wife's lover.

Pnin is obviously shocked by this turn of events; he was, after all, so close to what he thought might be happiness and tranquility. When all the guests leave, Pnin decides to wash the dishes and tidy up. At this point, Nabokov inserts an episode charged with both high tragedy and unique optimism. Among the dishes that Pnin lowers into the kitchen sink is an antique aquamarine bowl of exceptional value and beauty, a real piece of art, given to him by Victor. While washing the dishes, Pnin

> groped under the bubbles, around the goblets, and under
> the melodious bowl, for any piece of forgotten silver—and
> retrieved a nutcracker. Fastidious Pnin rinsed it, and was
> wiping it, when the leggy thing somehow slipped out of
> the towel and fell like a man from a roof. He almost
> caught it—his fingertips actually came into contact with
> it in midair, but this only helped to propel it into the trea-
> sure-concealing foam of the sink, where an excruciating
> crack of breaking glass followed upon the plunge. (p. 171)

But the aquamarine bowl is intact; it was just a goblet that broke.

The implications and the symbolic meaning of this passage are central: art always remains intact; art is able to survive any crucial event. The survival of this art object signals Pnin's own survival and his transcendence of exile.

As Edmund Wilson saw, *Pnin* is the novel through which Nabokov finally reached the great American public. The American-Russian writer's art as well as the artist himself did make this precious contact and survive. Pnin is on the run again, but he is alive on some other campus, in a different house, still trying to puzzle out the elaborate pattern of the wallpaper in his Russian nursery. He is still learning how to balance the vertical and horizontal planes of his existence, while Nabokov is sitting back in an armchair, in a house that does not belong to him, reading the galleys of a novel called *Pnin*.

Three

I. B. SINGER

The Convergence of Art and Faith

Shosha

> *Binele, I won't abandon you. I swear by the*
> *soul of your mother.*
> I. B. Singer, "The Lecture"
>
> *I will make it so you will live forever.*
> I.B. Singer, *Shosha*

In 1967, in the December issue of *Playboy* magazine, I. B. Singer published one of his best short stories, "The Lecture." This short piece, included later in the collection *The Seance and Other Stories*, can rightfully stand as an epigraph for the Yiddish writer's entire literary production. The theme of an exiled writer's efforts to relate his own past experience (as well as that of the entire Jewish nation) to the life of the present is a constant ingredient of both his novels and stories. "The Lecture" is a paradigm of it all.

The plot of the short story is as straightforward and uncomplicated as that of the majority of Singer's writings. But this simplicity will not deceive an attentive reader; it adds dimension and strength to the sincerity, agony, tragedy, and deep pain embedded in each word, sentence, and paragraph. I begin with this story not only because of its representative character in Singer's work, but because it bears a remarkable and revealing resemblance to Nabokov's novel *Pnin*, both in theme and in plot.

In the opening scenes of both the story and the novel, we encounter the main protagonists, N. and Pnin, two intellectuals, two exiled authors, who are on their way to deliver lectures to audiences who represent a vanished but still haunting past. (Nabokov would have been delighted at the coincidence that both he and Singer's character share the same initial letter in their names.) Letting the reader penetrate the minds of Pnin and N., the writers reveal an initially startling similarity in the patterns of their thinking as well as in the nature of the problems that obsess them. Both Pnin and N. are worried about their money, their passports, and their manuscripts, which, needless to say, get lost on their way to exotic, faraway places. Both find it necessary to describe in detail their journey on the train, meticulously pointing out all the complications that befall them. They share identical feelings of isolation and alienation from their fellow travelers. But, most important, the two exiled writers are constantly brooding about their past experiences, which they thought they would be able to leave behind them when forced to leave Eastern Europe. Both Pnin and N. return often in their reminiscences to the Holocaust and Stalin's purges—the two catastrophes that have so radically changed the course of events in the twentieth century. Both direct as well as indirect encounters with these events played a major role in turning the two writers into exiles. It is not just a mere coincidence, therefore, that both should respond similarly to the European cataclysms that had disrupted their personal lives and altered the destinies of their people.

Singer and Nabokov use identical techniques to convey the sense of tragedy, a permanent companion to exiled intellectuals, over the loss of a world that is no more. Scenes of the present invariably evoke Pnin's and N.'s reminiscences. Frequently, both in the story and in the novel, the distinctions between past and present are blurred, and it remains the reader's task, in order to gain a better insight into the texts, to distinguish the two planes of existence that are so intricately intertwined and often indiscernible. But, as I hope to show, it is even more important for the two protagonists to be able not only to disentangle their experiences but also to balance past and present, thus establishing an equilibrium that will ensure their intellectual survival.

While waiting to board his train, N. feels alienated from his fellow travelers: "It was as if they knew nothing of the existence of world problems or eternal questions, as though they had never heard of death, sickness, war, poverty, betrayal, or even such troubles as missing a train, losing a ticket, or being robbed."[1] In this condensed statement, Singer makes a veiled reference to a horrible past that means nothing to N.'s new countrymen, Americans.

N.'s lecture is to deal with the future of Yiddish as a language. He is going to argue for optimism about the survival of this language, despite the fact that the Holocaust reduced by several million the number of its speakers. As a result of the Holocaust, Yiddish has, paradoxically, turned into a holy language, *lashon hakodesh*, thus taking the place of Hebrew, which became the everyday language in the state of Israel. Although N.'s predictions are going to be optimistic, he has doubts about his presentation; the closer the train brings him to his destination the deeper his doubts become. His mental changes are paralleled by the physical changes on the train. The feelings of comfort and the relaxing heat of the compartment give way to restlessness and the discomforting cold. When the train suddenly breaks down and the freezing winter temperatures begin to penetrate its every corner, the narrator's thoughts turn more often to his past, to Poland, to the people he will never see again. The sense of isolation becomes more acute; the only means he has to warm himself is the bottle of cognac that he was wise enough to bring with him from New York.

It is past midnight when the train finally pulls into the depot. The station is abandoned and covered by a white carpet of deep snow. The cold is miserable; N. is on the verge of despair. But suddenly he notices two figures, whom he instinctively approaches. The two women, mother and daughter, are the only ones who waited for the renowned Yiddish writer to arrive. Hardly have they exchanged greetings, when the mother, a "lame woman," is already talking about dreadful and traumatic experiences in the displaced persons' camps, relating in frightful detail the fate of her family. The younger woman, Binele, who is herself survivor of Auschwitz, tries to calm her mother. But the daughter's admonitions are of no avail—nothing can silence her mother, who was so impatiently waiting for the great Yiddish author precisely in order to pour her heart out. Her behavior implies that she places high hopes on N., since only a true artist is able to perceive and fully comprehend the grief which has never ceased to torture her.

Survivors, Singer suggests, cannot be quiet, and even when they are, their silence sometimes assumes more meaning than volumes written by the most eloquent writers. N. knows that it is his duty to listen and to absorb everything this tragic figure, this miraculously saved remnant of the past, has to relate to him and, through him, to the entire world. The blood-chilling stories do nothing to relieve his feelings of cold. The frost becomes nearly unbearable to him. This sensation of cold is intensified when N. enters the tiny, run-down house of the two survivors where he is to spend the night. As if the cold were not enough to make him miserable, N. suddenly becomes aware that he has lost his manuscript; he is not even sure whether he still has his citizenship papers; he feels as if he is getting pneumonia. Suddenly he becomes conscious of painfully familiar odors that assail him from all the corners of the little house that evoke images from the past better forgotten. N. does not even try to fight them off; like Pnin, he cannot forget the unforgettable; he cannot and probably does not want to run away from the impressions that the old woman's Holocaust stories make on him.

Failing to overcome insomnia, unable to warm up even under three layers of blankets, N. tries consciously to get the feeling of what it meant to live through the Nazi atrocities: "Well, let me imagine that I remained under Hitler in wartime. Let me get some taste of that, too" (pp. 76–77). And as if to answer his call for a complete identification with the survivors, fate plays a foul trick on the narrator; in the middle of the night the old woman suddenly dies. Terror strikes N. when he hears the heartbreaking, horror-filled lamentations of the daughter. *Now*, indeed, he seems to comprehend fully what it means to be a victim, misunderstood, forgotten, ignored by the entire world. A neighbor, when solicited for help, is quite indifferent to what has just happened one floor below his apartment. Not only does he fail to grasp the tragedy of the situation, but, in addition, he cannot or does not want to understand English. Singer here suggests that the present circumstances are analogous to those in the past; then there was no common language between the victim and the outside world, a world that did nothing to prevent the destruction of almost a whole nation.

This event in the present gives rise to N.'s thoughts about the past: "My years in America seemed to have been swept away by that one night and I was taken back, as though by magic, to my worst days in Poland, to the bitterest crisis of my life" (p. 81). The present is inseparable from the past. The death of this survivor indicates to the narrator, and to Singer as well, that a true artist cannot keep silent about the events of the past, that it is his moral duty to relate the Holocaust experience to those who care to know. This is the legacy that N. inherits from the old woman. At once, looking at the tattoed number on Binele's wrist, he proudly accepts the bittersweet burden of the rememberer. At the deathbed of yet another Nazi victim, N. gives his solemn oath to the six million Jewish people, who cannot, unfortunately, be among his readers and listeners: "'Binele, I won't abandon you. I swear by the soul of your mother'" (p. 83). And only at this moment does the cold finally let up and the snow begin to melt. The artist, thus, becomes the only true intermediary between the past and present.

I. B. Singer did not break the promise made by his double to Binele and her mother. He knew that the delayed death of a miraculously saved soul was an unequivocal message to a Yiddish writer, an outcry not to forget, a plea to commemorate through art not only the tragic events of the past but also the endurance and the vital powers of the Jewish people. Singer's novel *Shosha* can be justly regarded as his protagonist's fulfillment of the commitment he made at the deathbed of Binele's mother. N.'s pledge to never forget resounds in Aaron Gredinger's oath to Shosha to remember her forever, not to "forget anything," and to "make it so that [she'll] live forever."[2]

Prior to being published as a full-length novel in 1978, *Shosha* was serialized in the New York–based Yiddish newspaper, *The Forward,* under the title *Soul Expeditions.* (Why the book's title was changed will become clear later.) The name Shosha is familiar to most of Singer's readers: he has devoted an entire chapter to this "image" of his past in his compilation of children's stories *A Day of Pleasure*; he also mentions her several times in his memoir, *In My Father's Court*. His insistence on having this character reappear time and again in his literary works should put Singer's reader on alert. Fortunately, Singer is not writing a detective novel, and he has no intention of keeping the reader in suspense in regard to Shosha's frequent appearances in his fiction. In the novel, Betty, one of Aaron's numerous mistresses, asks him what he sees in Shosha that he should be so drawn to her. His answer is curt and defeatingly sincere: he sees in Shosha himself, that is, his past, which, as becomes clear later, is inseparable from his present existence.

Shosha is not a simple novel. One can wholeheartedly sympathize with Aaron's agonies when writing his play, *The Lubomir Maiden*, which, according to his own admission, contained a "magical theme—like the Torah, it seemed to possess seventy different faces" (p. 58). *Shosha* too is a multifaceted book, a large canvas, that betrays the author's ambition to incorporate into it the many elements scattered through all his novels and stories, as well as to add new dimenions to his literary activity. *Shosha* summarizes what he has done in his entire literary career; in other words, the novel is yet another fictionalized memoir of Isaac Bashevis Singer. Like Nabokov's *Mary*, *Shosha* is a novel about the birth of an artist.

Biography and fiction are nearly indistinguishable in *Shosha*. Edward Alexander, in his full-length book, *I. B. Singer*, points out that *Shosha* is Singer's first novel published in English that is written as a first-person narrative.[3] This fact, coupled with the reader's awareness of the publication of *A Young Man in Search of Love*, a nonfictional Singer memoir issued almost simultaneously with *Shosha*, adds to the impression that *Shosha* is a fictional autobiography. Indeed, when one compares the memoir and the novel, one cannot help noticing how much of what is in the memoir finds its way into the novel.

Both the book and the memoir address themselves to questions invariably posed by young, aspiring artists. What is the purpose of literature? What should one write about? How is one to translate into writing the creative powers one possesses? The list of inquiries can go on endlessly; these questions are ageless. But what makes the complexities of the problems raised by Singer's doubles even more pointed is the reader's singular awareness of the historical circumstances under which a Singerian artist has to function.

Most of the events in *Shosha* take place in the nineteen twenties and thirties, that is, the years between the two world wars. The place is Poland; the main characters are Jews. Hasidism, a Jewish mystical movement founded in Poland in about 1750 in opposition to rationalism and ritual laxity, and the movement of Haskalah or Enlightenment become the two poles of thinking within the Jewish population of Poland. There are those who advocate the traditional way of life, that is, the way of life to which Polish Jews were accustomed during the eight centuries of exile in that country. On the other hand, there emerges an ever-growing segment of mostly young people who want to leave the ghettos and whose search for a new identity places them in extreme oppositon to their upbringing. They want worldliness, assimilation, enlightenment.

To be sure, neither of these groups is homogeneous in its demands and visions of the future. Even the Hasidim, proponents of the traditional, are not like their fathers who established the tradition. Bashele, Shosha's mother, sums it up this way: "'There are no such Jews anymore. Even Hasidim dress like dandies today—cutaway gaberdines, polished boots'" (p. 78). The divergences among the enlightened Jews are no less noticeable. For some, Soviet Russia and its socioeconomic structure is the only model to follow; Stalin is often portrayed as a savior of the world from the evils that beset it. Others advocate total assimilation, announcing thus the inconsequentiality of the two thousand years of Jewish life in the Diaspora. Yet another group calls upon the Jews to return to the Holy Land and build a state that will express the new Jewish identity and consciousness.

But all of these impassioned theories of change and newness are overshadowed by constant feelings of doubt and ambivalence. Somewhere deep in their minds and hearts, these people are conscious of the futility of their efforts to escape their heritage. Aaron's pointed observation aptly expresses the essence of the state of mind of those around him: "We are running away and Mount Sinai runs after us. This chase has made us sick and mad" (p. 255). The significance of this statement is heightened when one rememebers that the sinister shadow of Nazi Germany has by this time covered nearly all Europe. In consequence of this, Polish Jewry feels that it is gradually becoming entrapped between the forces of Polish Panslavic anti-Semitism and Hitler's destructive force that threatens its annihilation.

It is in these times and under such circumstances that Aaron Greidinger firmly decides to become a writer and devote his life to art. Like Singer, the son of an Orthodox rabbi, Aaron "was brought up on three dead languages—Hebrew, Aramaic, Yiddish . . . and a culture that developed in Babylon: the Talmud" (p. 1). In this very first sentence of the novel, Singer points out the two problems that are inseparable companions of any transplanted writer, namely, language and exile. The influence of his home, deeply steeped in tradition, is apparent in all Singer's writings. Aaron's home is identical to Singer's. From an early age the boy had a strong urge to write. He once confided to Shosha, who lived in the same apartment house on Krochmalna Street, that he "was writing a book" (p. 7). As a teenager, Aaron was a voracious reader; his reading had to be done in secret because his father would not tolerate any writing outside of the realm of the Pentateuch, the Talmud, and the Mishna. Aaron, though, indulged in worldly books, written by such (to his father) sinister figures as Dostoyevsky, Spinoza, Schopenhauer. The young man was searching for the answer to the eternal question of how one can remain a Jew and be worldly at the same time.

Both Singer and his double, Aaron, were very much involved in the intellectual Yiddish milieu of Warsaw. As a member of the writers' club, Aaron had a chance to meet with older as well as younger aspiring artists, all of whom were posing similar questions. These encounters, though primarily futile, taught Aaron one thing: he should be different, he should be above the gossip and trivialities in which his pseudointellectual colleagues indulged. They, he understood, could not become the models after whom he might fashion himself. Aaron felt that he was not tailored to write works that would advance political slogans or adhere to the principles of "socialist realism" then in vogue among writers with procommunist inclinations. Neither was the young man overanxious to cram his future books with messages that might suit the needs of the hour. This is not to say that he did not understand the dangers of Nazism and the urgency to stand up against it; he was aware of the calls of politically conscious critics to expose Hitlerism as well as their insistence on writing plays on the "need of resistance by the Jewish masses, not dramas that brought back superstition of the Middle Ages" (p. 115). Literature, according to Aaron, should be above politics; to mix the two was not his inclination, not yet. On the other hand, this son of a rabbi was not willing to conform to the views of the hedonists and escapists who argued that the only things Jews wanted to see in the books of contemporary authors were trash and sex.

Caught in the middle of this controversy, Aaron remains creatively impotent, chastising himself for wasting his time and indulging in daydreaming and sexual escapades. He often thinks of suicide. Yet despite his self-destructive urges, Aaron never abandons his desire to define to himself, as well as to others, his role as an artist. "What kind of writer was I," he frequently asks himself. "I hadn't published a single book . . . I . . . imagined I had written a work that would startle the world. But what could startle the world? No crime, no misery, no sexual perversion, no madness. Twenty million people had perished in the Great War, and here the world was preparing for another conflagration. What could I write about that wasn't already known? A new style? Every experiment with words quickly turned into a collection of mannerisms" (p. 25). This statement not only illuminates the workings of an artist's mind; it also makes the reader understand Aaron's ahistorical view of history. On another occasion, he reinforces this view by defining the history of the world as a long chain of wars, a version of Pnin's assertion that the history of mankind is the history of pain.

Indeed, what could a writer like Aaron write about if history (and consequently suffering) repeats itself with such a morbid regularity? He was conscious of and well versed in the history of the Jews; he could not fail to see that their prospects at present were grim, to say the least. Nevertheless, his mind was set—he had to write even though it might mean the repetition of old truths and old ideas.

The people with whom Aaron surrounded himself were not helpful. Most of them were resigned to their deaths. Morris Feitelzohn, Aaron's self-appointed mentor and patron who chose the exile of Poland over the exile of America and who preached hedonism as the only escape from the burdens of the past and the futility of the present, was of no assistance to Aaron. His cynicism had no appeal to the young man who vehemently rejected the older man's advice to give the Jews what they wanted most—"sex, Torah, Revolution." Betty, the cosmopolitan actress who crosses and recrosses the Atlantic in search of her identity, uses a double-edged sword in her relationship with Aaron, whose mistress she eventually becomes. On the one hand, she encourages him to write and shows genuine feeling for the young man; on the other hand, she distorts and destroys the play he is writing for her, which is the result of numerous sleepless nights and hard creative labor. She is unable to understand that her constant prattle about suicide as well as her insatiable sexual desires tend to stifle rather than revive the young man's artistic urges. And then there is Celia, a middle-aged woman, surrounded by riches and art objects, pampered by her immature husband, used by Feitelzohn, her idol and lover. Celia's entire time is spent either in a dimly lit, cozy living room or in the embraces of her entertainers, Aaron among them, brooding ceaselessly over death and suicide. What could she offer Aaron? Inspiration?— probably not. Her body?—it did not differ much from others that he had known. Solace?—in death, maybe.

Even more destructive to Aaron's writing career were the predictions of these characters about the future of the Jews in Poland. Betty and Celia, Feitelzohn and Haiml, Sam and Tekla are constantly warning the young writer that total annihilation of the Polish Jewry is on its way. Their predictions of the Holocaust indicate the homogeneity of thought among representatives of different strata of Polish society. Here is Morris: "'Tsutsik, don't stay in Poland. A holocaust is coming here that will be worse than in Chmielnitsky's time. If you can get a visa—even a tourist visa—escape!'" (p. 151). (These are the words of a self-appointed priest of the hedonist temple.) Haiml, Celia's husband who preaches the doctrines of Poale Zion, according to which Jews have to forget about the thousands of years in exile and go to Palestine, also urges Aaron to leave, though he himself behaves contrary to the principles he is so wholeheartedly embracing. "'If you have a chance to escape from here, don't wait,'" he admonishes Aaron. "'We're caught between Hitler and Stalin. Whichever invades the country will bring a cataclysm'" (p. 64).

Aaron feels the need to justify his immobility and inertia. He witnesses Hitler's occupation of one country after another: he is bitter about the Allies assuming a "wait and see" position; he clearly perceives that all these developments leave the Jews of Poland without any hope. "But running away," he asserts, "and leaving at bay those who were dear to me was not in my nature" (p. 120). Given his resolution, not even the businesslike exhortations of Sam Dreiman can be of any avail to him. "'Things will not end well in Poland,'" Sam predicts. "'That beast Hitler will soon come with his Nazis. There'll be a great war. Americans will lend a hand and they'll do what they did in the last war, but before that the Nazis will attack the Jews and there'll be nothing but grief for you here'" (pp. 155–56).

After reading these warnings, the paradox embedded in them is clear: these people clearly perceived the grief Hitler's inevitable occupation would bring, yet they didn't leave in time to prevent their own destruction.

Celia provides at least a partial answer to this paradox. She is also among those who embody ambivalent attitudes toward Aaron. On the one hand, she urges Aaron to escape and avoid committing "literary suicide," but she herself is determined to die in Poland rather than attempt a new start as an exile in still another country: "'I keep myself going only with the force of inertia, or call it what you will. I don't want to go to a foreign land and lie sick in some hotel room or hospital. I want to die in my own room. I don't want to rest in a strange cemetery'" (p. 244–45). Exile is what most frightens these people; they are tired of being wandering Jews. Betty, the actress constantly on the run, speaks for all of them when she says that "the sad truth is that for me there isn't *one* place in the world where I feel at home" (p. 132). And yet, these homeless people beg Aaron to escape. Consciously or subconsiously, all of them believe in Aaron's artistic

genius. They urge him to write because by writing he will survive and atone for the sins that resulted in their exile. The frequent, and only slightly camouflaged admissions of the sinful
existence they lead testify to their awareness that they are following in the path of their forefathers, committing the very idolatry that caused the expulsion of the Jews from the land of Israel. Writing is seen by them as a means to transcend alienation
and estrangement from tradition. On the other hand, these
people, who have resigned themselves to death, need someone to
record and take account of their lives. They desire a rememberer
who will through his writings make future generations more
aware of the Jewish Polish milieu and of the fate they already
anticipate at the hands of the Nazis. Celia and Haiml, Aaron and
Dora, Morris and Betty—all of them are conscious of abandoning the true path of Judaism, committing thus the sin that
brought upon them the curse of exile. Aaron is an artist, a writer,
whom they choose as their intermediary between righteousness
and evil, between the past and the present. They never doubt his
literary genius; they believe that he will not fail to perform the
holy duty with which they have entrusted him—to intercede for
them and to commemorate their lives in his writings.

But Aaron does not flee, not yet. Before he escapes he must
know exactly what he is leaving behind; he has to have a precise,
nearly scientific knowledge of the society he abandons. Superficial knowledge of the past cannot satisfy the young man; he
must get to its core, learn its nature, understand its inner workings. He has to touch it, to smell it, to see it as it is and as it was
for hundreds of years. At this point in his life Shosha, the ageless, physically deformed, blonde, blue-eyed girl with a short
nose and thin lips—the girl who spoke the pure Yiddish of Krochmalna Street and who, as Aaron puts it, "in her own fashion denied death" (p. 91)—begins to work miracles on the artist. None
of Aaron's enlightened friends can explain why Aaron is so drawn
to Shosha; later, when he decides to marry the cripple, all of
them are shocked because they see his action as a denial of common sense, and a fatal obstacle to leaving Poland. Aaron is hard
put to explain this step; all he can say to his stubborn inter-
rogators is that Shosha "is a girl from my childhood. We were
neighbors at No. 10 Krochmalna Street. Later I went away and

for many years" (p. 136). Aaron fails to finish the sentence, and it remains the reader's task to complete it by closely following the development of the events of the novel.

Shosha, as later becomes clear, represents to the young artist the coherence and integrity of the Jewish people and their past. Even while absent from Krochmalna Street, Aaron did not forget this girl; the memories of her were deeply embedded in his mind, only to surface later and drastically change his behavior and actions. He often dreamed of Shosha, and in his dreams the two were invariably together joined by a miraculous bond.

Prior to achieving the oneness with Shosha that brings him the peace of mind necessary for his creative powers to return, Aaron has to undergo a crisis of self-doubt and resignation. But once he decides to be reunited with his childhood sweetheart, with his past, it is easier for him to shake off the destructive influences of his friends and mistresses. He abandons Dora because of her reluctance to give up her utopian communist views; Aaron cannot identify with totalitarian regimes. He is not just against communism but against all other "isms" as well. He finally finds the strength to reject Betty and Celia and to be free from the intrigues and slime into which they dragged him. Feitelzohn's theories do not appeal to him any more; he sees clearly that Morris created them solely to escape reality rather than to admit the meaninglessness of his existence. Aaron is beginning to understand that he "has thrown away four thousand years of Jewishness and exchanged it for meaningless literature, Yiddishism, Feitelzohnism" (p. 257). It also takes the sharp razor blade of an anti-Semitic Polish barber held at his throat as well as the prophetic voice of his dead father, speaking to him in the most crucial moment of his life, to rouse him from lethargy and move him to transform his life.

Leaving the barber shop, where he is mistaken for a gentile and therefore privileged to hear the most hideous anti-Semitic pronouncements, Aaron is shaking with fear, disgust, and shame. "I began to race," he recalls, "not knowing in what direction I was going. *No, I wouldn't stay in Poland! I'd leave at any price!* (p. 164). Having made this decision, though not knowing yet what direction to take, Aaron now fully understands the admonitions of his father whose tradition he had denied, the admonitions earlier conveyed to him in a sudden vision of the old man accompanied by the thunderous voice of the righteous:

> "Run!" a voice cried within me. "You'll sink into a slime
> from which you'll never be able to get out. They'll drag
> you into the abyss!" . . . "Don't shame me, your mother
> and your holy ancestors! All your deeds are noted in
> heaven." . . . "Heathen! Betrayer of Israel! See what hap-
> pens when you deny the Almighty! 'You shall utterly detest
> it and you shall utterly abhor it, for it is a cursed thing.'"
> (p. 158)

And run Aaron does, with his first stop at Bashele's apartment on Krochmalna Street, where the pure and virginal Shosha was patiently waiting for him.

Only when he is back on the street where he grew up, reunited with his past, does Aaron begin to attain some spiritual calm and tranquility. Only when he becomes one with Shosha, Singer seems to imply, do his creative powers return to him and enable him to write a novel that miraculously integrates the feuding Jewish camps, the traditional and the enlightened. Singer's intentions are clear at this point: literature and art can perform miracles where other intellectual institutions fail.[4]

Clearly Shosha inspires Aaron; she resurrects for him a past that the two once so happily shared. However, Shosha also threatens to endanger the writer's further creative existence. She provides a temporary, though necessary respite by recreating his past. It is true that awareness of the past is a required condition for Aaron's creative powers to be sustained. But to ignore and blot out the present will jeopardize his intellectual survival. He has to learn how to balance the two.

With Shosha's generous help, Aaron finally acquires the exact and so persistently sought knowledge of his past. Not only has he learned how to avoid being paralyzed by it, he has also learned how to benefit from the past's life-giving powers. Now, reunited with Shosha and having paid tribute to his past by his literary endeavors in the Polish exile, Aaron can run and fight for his survival without feelings of guilt for betraying those dear to him.

The Victorian epilogue of the novel provides additional information about its main characters. Aaron Greidinger, the now acclaimed and distinguished American Yiddish author, is brought by Singer to visit the land of Israel, where, thirteen years after leaving Poland, he meets Haiml, the only survivor of his days of youth. It is through his account to Haiml that we learn about Shosha's death as well as about Aaron's exodus from Poland. The two, together with other refugees, were nearly out of the country when Shosha suddenly fell to the ground and died. Her death had a twofold effect on Aaron: it caused him much grief, but at the same time, it made his road to freedom much easier. In the literal sense, Aaron did not succeed. But, paradoxically, he became the beneficiary of Shosha's death. He inherited from her the knowledge that otherwise would have been lost to himself and therefore to his readers. Shosha presented Aaron with a store of memories that enrich the experiences of his present life and enable him to memorialize the past of the Jewish people of Eastern Europe and their lives in his many novels and stories. His works will always be a reminder of a world that is no more.

THE SLAVE

> *After the doings of the land of Egypt, wherein ye dwelt, shall ye not do: and after the doings of the land of Canaan, whither I bring you, shall ye not do: neither shall ye walk in their ordinances.*
> Leviticus, 18:3

> *Now he knew what he was: a branch torn from his trunk.*
> I. B. Singer, *The Slave*

Since its publication in 1962, *The Slave* has been one of I. B. Singer's most widely read novels. It has enthralled the minds and hearts of readers and critics alike. Had Singer been the author of only this book, he would have left his imprint on the literature of the twentieth century. The particularity and the universality of the novel's theme and characters, the timelessness of its ideas, its masterful recreation of man's eternal odyssey toward happiness and self-fulfillment are among the achievements of *The Slave*. That literary critics have wrestled with the multitude of possible readings of *The Slave* is an additional testimony to the complexity and genius of Singer's novel, which, like many other artistic masterpieces, can only be approached from one or another angle but never grasped in its totality.

Edward Alexander's observation that the novel has a "vast backward and forward reference"[5] may help one understand why it is so difficult to write about *The Slave* without digressing into theology, ethics, and philosophy, as many commentators of the book indeed do. His statement that the novel "looks backward to the Bible, especially to the warfare between nascent Judaism and ancient idolatry, and forward to the Holocaust,"[6] may, to a certain extent, clarify Susan Sontag's uncertainty about defining the book as either a conventional or modern composition. She chooses the latter.[7] The breadth of the novel and its numerous allusions to phenomena that lie beyond the text make critics come to diametrically opposite conclusions as to the intentions of the writer as well as to the behavioral motivations of the book's main protagonist, Jacob. One may see his existence as meaningful and self-fulfilling,[8] while another categorically asserts that "his very existence is nullity."[9]

I prefer to treat this novel as a classical illustration of the problems of exile. The novel works as a kind of laboratory; it is equipped with intricate machinery to record the slightest nuances and changes in the condition not only of a single one of its transplanted characters but also of a whole transplanted nation. Many of Singer's characters, as I pointed out in my discussion of *Shosha*, are aware, subconsciously, of the reason for their exile. But Jacob, in *The Slave*, straightforwardly expresses this reason without any hesitation or doubt when he patiently tries to explain the principles of Judaism to his future mistress and wife, Wanda:

> "Why aren't the Jews still in their country?"
> "Because they transgressed."
> "What did they do?"
> "They bowed down to idols and stole from the poor."[10]

Furthermore, only in this novel does Singer depart from his much cherished path of ambiguity and offer a concrete way to transcend exile and shake off the bondage of slavery.

Allusions to the Bible are abundant in this novel, and Singer organizes the names of numerous biblical characters as well as the events in which they were involved into a coherent pattern. After all, the Bible can be viewed in part as the story of the Jewish people's constant endeavors to transcend its exile. Almost all of the articles written about *The Slave* draw a convincing parallel between the exodus of Jacob and that of his ancestors.

Jacob, according to his own defintion, is a Jew, a teacher, and a survivor of the Chmielnicki massacre. As a result, this tall, blue-eyed man with long brown hair and a brown beard finds himself uprooted and violently torn away from his native town, Josefov. He suspects that his entire family has been mercilessly slaughtered. Through some inexplicable miracle, Jacob's life is spared, but he is sold into slavery by brigands to Jan Bzick, a Gazda in a godforsaken, semibarbarian village. Jacob now becomes an exile and a slave. In his thoughts he often associates himself with another exile, the biblical Samson, but unlike his ancient counterpart who chooses death rather than life among the despicable Philistines, Jacob manages to fight off the feelings of resignation that often visit him in the solitude of sleepless nights and to survive with dignity and a sense of great accomplishment.

Although the novel consists of three parts and accommodates a multitude of minor and major characters, Jacob is never left out of the spectrum of the author's attention. At times the book indeed resembles an experimental novel by Zola, in which a character is placed into different situations and is under the constant observation of a detached, objective creator. All his reactions and behavioral deviations from the expected norms are scrupulously recorded and left to the subjective analyses of a subjective reader. Singer, though, cannot be an indifferent creator since he himself shares not only Jacob's fate but that of his people as well. Therefore, all the resolutions at which Jacob might arrive will have been at least partially shared by the writer himself. It is difficult to disregard Singer's often reiterated admission and insistence that "I am all of my characters."[11]

In my discussion of Nabokov's novel *Mary,* I pointed out that the Russian writer creates a chain of cagelike images, with the parent cage being exile itself, and has his protagonist, Ganin, pass from one cage to another, acquiring in the process of his journey the qualities to transcend exile and assure, through art and intellect, his survival. A similar device is employed by Singer as well, though on a loftier and a more distinctly outlined plane. As with Ganin, the reader first encounters Jacob when he is confined within the walls of his first cage, that is, during his exile in the community of the beastly Polish peasants. It is only through the reminiscences of both the Russian and Jewish characters that the past experiences of the two and the intricate workings of fate that caused their present situation come to light.

After finally being delivered from his first cage, Jacob moves into another one, his hometown of Josefov, where the now liberated slave feels again alienated and isolated from the community that he once called his own. Jacob's cohabitation with Wanda in the Pilitz congregation of unfriendly fellow Jews becomes yet another link in the series of confinements the author makes him pass through. But this cage differs drastically from the previous ones—Jacob is not alone in his search for the essence of human existence; now he has a partner, Wanda, for whom exile becomes as real as it is for Jacob. Wanda's exile among the Jews is a mirror image of Jacob's exile among her countrymen. Only when the two become sole possessors of the experiences and consequences of exile and are able to identify fully with each other's transplanted state can they finally be considered an integral unit, separable only by death. There are yet two more stages through which Jacob must pass. In a few brief passages, the reader learns about Jacob's twenty-year-long settlement in the Holy Land, which is followed by an equally short narrative of his return to exile. To see what consitutes this enigmatic force that drives Jacob from one cage to another, I will have to enter the cages that generate it, dwelling in the first the longest.

We may recall that the opening sentence of Singer's *Shosha* introduces two main problems, namely, language and the essence of exile, issues that constantly obsess transplanted artists. In the very first pages of *The Slave*, Singer deals with the same questions. As one might recall after reading Nabokov, the discussion of language and exile is invariably accompanied by a study of memory, the particular memory of a displaced person. Singer follows the same pattern. It seems evident that gaining a deep insight into the workings of memory is a matter of utmost importance to an exiled writer. This faculty enables him to recreate artistically his past; in order to survive, he must come to terms with this past. No one, as Freud ponts out again and again, can free himself from his past without causing himself emotional damage; and this is particularly true of exiles. The past contains, as Freud asserts, the ingredients of one's future.

Memory in both Nabokov's and Singer's novels has the same attributes: it is highly selective and fragmented; it is the foundation of the characters' artistic imaginations. Memory helps them to restore part of their existence; this reconstruction of the past is a condition for their survival.

Jacob suffers when he tries to recall certain events of his past; he accuses memory of playing "hide and seek" with him. He bitterly laments his failures and calls memory a "miser." His perseverance, though, is limitless: "It [memory] did not like to give, but if one remained stubborn and did not cease asking, it would pay out even more than what was demanded. Never left in peace, it would at last return all that had been deposited within" (pp. 37–38). If conscious and willed memory does not help to bring about the desired results, then the subconscious part of one's mind comes to its assistance. Jacob often dreams, and in his dreams he frequently sees himself back in Josefov, teaching the Talmud to the young men of his native town.

When we first encounter Jacob, he appears to be a lonely and frustrated man who understands both the irony and the tragedy of the daily repeated prayer, "Thou hast not made me a slave." The irony is that the worshipper is physically a slave, and as a slave he *still* repeats the prayer every morning with the hope that the tragedy of his slavery will soon come to an end. At this point of the novel, Jacob has not yet understood the full meaning of this prayer. He knows what it asserts, but he has no *conscious* awareness of what it demands. He is not able to penetrate the hidden call for protest against one's status quo that this prayer contains: if you are a slave at present, it does not mean that you must remain a slave. The development of the novel's story will show Jacob's progress from a subconscious to a conscious understanding of this utterance, an understanding that will move him to action and, finally, to freedom as well.

Slavery presupposes losing self-control and submitting to a dominating influence. Freedom, then, demands regaining self-control and becoming independent. Jacob is neither totally free nor totally enslaved. Physically, he is indeed a bondman forced into bondage; he has no control over this. On the other hand, he stubbornly rejects the heathen influence that the surrounding world is trying to impose upon him. What are the means that Jacob chooses to revolt against his present situation?

One of Jacob's main concerns is with language. Four years is a long time to be away from the linguistic atmosphere of Yiddish. Our protagonist makes every effort to retain the knowledge of his native tongue, since this knowledge makes him different from those around him; moreover, Yiddish remains one of the important links with his past and his people. To remember the language Jacob goes to the extreme (which might be called insanity by some) of speaking Yiddish "to the cows, to himself even" (p. 4). The only reason for doing this, as Jacob points out, is "not to forget Yiddish" (p. 4).

Not to have a language, Singer implies, is to be reduced to the level of brute animals. He illustrates this by his description of the peasant women who surround Jacob: "They behaved little better than beasts. In his presence they relieved themselves. . . . 'Lay me,' a girl would shamelessly demand. . . . These women were unclean, and had vermin in their clothes and elflocks in their hair; often their skins were covered with rashes and boils, they ate field rodents and rotting carcasses of fowls. *Some of them could scarcely speak Polish* [my emphasis], grunted like animals, screamed and laughed madly" (p. 9).

We may also recall at this point that what sets Wanda, Jacob's mistress-to-be, apart from the rest of the womenfolk of the village is her good command of Polish. "Often Wanda herself was amazed by the words that issued from her lips. At times they had the pithiness and wit of a bishop's talk. Basha and her mother gaped. Jan Bzick stirred and murmured something" (p. 30). Wanda's knowledge makes her different from the rest of the family as well. In addition, it enables her to communicate with Jacob. When with Jacob, Wanda exhibits a genuine fascination with words, although she at times laments that he uses "strange" and incomprehensible words that make her feel different from him too.

The trilevel linguistic hierarchy that Singer establishes has far-reaching implications. The beastly peasants are obviously beyond redemption. Wanda, through her constant effort to refine her language, has a good chance for salvation. Indeed, as we discover later in the novel, it is largely through her perseverance in her studies of Yiddish that Wanda finds a key to the secrets of the Jewish faith and understands its supremacy over carnal love. Jacob, for his part, by retaining his native tongue, avoids the pitfalls of becoming "one of them"; language is to a great extent responsible for his spiritual survival.

I. B. Singer does not advocate ethnocentricity. There is no sin, he implies, in knowing the language of the stranger; but without good knowledge of a native tongue, one may not perceive the intricacies of language and, consequently, the thoughts of others. In his childhood, Jacob studied Polish; his captivity improves it to such an extent that he can easily pass for a gentile. Sometimes he even experiences difficulties in recalling the Yiddish names for certain objects. And yet, Yiddish is the language he wants to keep. For him, the preservation of the native tongue is not an aim in itself—what Jacob desires is to create in this medium. At this point, we come to yet another important element that ensures his survival in captivity.

Jacob, as we find out from his reminiscences, has always been considered a learned man. From early childhood he was interested in books; he was regarded as an intellectual in his community and even recommended to become the successor of Josefov's deceased rabbi. When he married his infantile wife he was "more interested in his father-in-law's library of rare books" (p. 52) than in the whinings of his ne'er-do-well wife, who was imposed on him against his will. Teaching young men the Talmud relieves him from this bond of a marriage. His urges to study have never subsided; when in captivity, they become stronger and grow into a near obsession. When Jacob finds himself among the Polish peasants, deprived of all the means to study, he initially becomes despondent. "Ceaselessly he prayed for death, he had even contemplated self-destruction" (p. 12). But being a pious Jew, Jacob knows that suicide is a grave sin in the canons of Judaism, which teach that when life seems unbearable there are still ways to avoid the state of utter resignation.

I. B. Singer does not let his hero down; he hastens to his help. What he offers Jacob becomes a universal remedy for many of his artist figures—salvation through art and intellect. What differentiates this Singerian offering from that of Nabokov is its close link to and often complete identification with Jewish faith. Art and Judaism not only coexist in Singer, they become one.

Like all displaced characters, Jacob cannot forget his past; moreover, he feels a strong need to remember it in order not to succumb to the dominating influences of his bondage. He is deprived of the physical objects that could identify him with his former existence: "He was without prayer shawl and phylacteries, fringed garment or holy book" (p. 6). But what he still has is something that no one can take away from him—he has a powerful memory and a true artistic imagination. The dilemma he faces is how to preserve this memory (that is, his past) and how to realize his artistic impulse. He desperately longs for pen and paper: "if he had pen and paper, he would have written down what came to him, but where were such things to be found here?" (p. 6). Writing thus becomes the ultimate necessity for this uprooted man. He knows that even without tools he still "must find a way to write everything down" (p. 38).

By describing in detail Jacob's strong artistic urges, Singer implies that nothing can stop such a man from creating art. Jacob was a man who "wrote in a fine bold hand" (p. 52), who was known to be a good singer, a gifted draftsman, an accomplished woodcarver, and a painter. How could an author fail such a character? He makes Jacob come to a sudden recognition that drastically changes his whole life. It occurs to Jacob that he could do what Moses had done. At this point art and Jewish faith converge. "'If Moses had been able to chisel the Ten Commandments onto stone,'" Jacob reasons with himself, "'why couldn't he?'" (p. 38). Once this crucial question is asked, action follows immediately. Pen and paper, manmade tools, are of no importance anymore. Nature gladly yields what man fails to provide.

All Jacob needs is stone and a carving instrument. After a brief search, he finds both—"The stone had been waiting ever since Creation" (p. 39).

When Jacob finally finds an outlet for his creative urges, nothing can stop him, not even his passion for Wanda. At this point of the novel, Singer provides the reader with a rare glimpse of the intricate workings of an artist's mind:

> What wonders issued from his [Jacob's] mind. He tortured memory and things he had long forgotten appeared. His was a never ending struggle with Purah, the lord of oblivion. In this battle force and persuasion were both necessary; patience was also required, but concentration was most important of all. Jacob sat midway between the barn and the rock, concealing himself with weeds and the branches of a midget pine. He mined within himself as men dig for treasure in the earth. It was slow work; he scratched sentences, fragments of sentences, single words into the stone. The Torah had not disappeared. It lay hidden in the nooks and crannies of his brain. (p. 40)

Jacob decides to engrave the 613 laws of the Torah, thus artistically recreating and commemorating not only his own past but also the collective past of his people, not an easy task. He has still to cope with the realities of the present, with the constant threats and dangers of physical destruction coming from the barbaric peasants.

Jacob's delicate situation among the villagers is analogous to the situation of Jews when they were wandering from one country into another, subjected to popular prejudice, looked upon as Christ-killers, and, as a result of this, turning into scapegoats when trouble visited their host country and its people. The historian Solo W. Baron makes a point of the "dichotomy that existed between popular concepts and the official teachings of the Church and State concerning Jews."[12] The term, "the perfidy of Jews," was taken literally by the general population, which inferred that the Jew was a born hypocrite and should, therefore, be destroyed. Dziobak, the priest of the village where Jacob is held captive, not only knows about the peasants' desire to rid themselves of the perfidious Jew, but, in addition, he encourages their murderous instincts. "'What's there to talk about?'" he says on one occasion. "'Climb up and dispose of him in God's name. I warned you, did I not, little brothers? I said he would bring only misfortune'" (p. 35). Jacob, for his part, is well aware that "as long as the village did not suffer from famine, epidemic, or fire, the Jew was to be left in peace" (p. 7). But should any of the above happen, he would be the first to incur blame. And yet, Jacob is not afraid; he has his art and faith to stand against the powers of destruction and oblivion. Even the cruel villagers are momentarily appeased by his beautiful singing of the psalms; they often fall prey to his enchanting narration of biblical stories. Both singing and storytelling, we have to remember, are art forms; they are integral parts of Jacob's larger art project, segments of his past, chapters from his engravings.

There are yet two more dangers to Jacob's survival. The first danger is Jacob's decreasing faith in God. He has constant disputes with the Almighty. He cannot understand why the Jewish people have had to endure so much suffering if they are the closest to God. It becomes difficult for him to explain the dichotomy between election and perpetual persecution. One minute he expresses his ardent belief in the Lord, and another he doubts his very existence. "He violently blamed the creator for forcing one very existence. "He violently blamed the creator for forcing one creature to annihilate another. Of all the questions he asked about the universe, he found this the most difficult" (p. 62). By having Jacob question his faith and directly confront God, Singer makes his character join in a long-standing tradition in Judaism and Jewish literature, in which the Lord, the partner in the Covenant, is brought to trial and harshly questioned as to the justice of his workings. There are numerous examples of such direct conflicts both in the Bible and postbiblical history as well. A few quotations illustrate this point. My first reference is to Habakkuk, a Hebrew prophet. Scholars do not unanimously agree on the time of his ministry or the origin of his name. The context of his writings suggests events that could have occurred between 586 B.C.E. and 550 B.C.E., that is, the fall of Jerusalem and the battle of Charchemish, respectively. Habakkuk straightforwardly questions God as to the equity of inflicting so much suffering

upon his people while its enemies rejoice in victory over the
Jews:

> How long, O Lord, shall I cry,
> And Thou wilt not hear?
> I cry out unto Thee in violence,
> And Thou wilt not save.
> Why dost Thou show me iniquity,
> And beholdest mischief?
> And why are spoiling and violence before me?
> So that there is strife, and contention ariseth?
> Therefore the law is slacked.
> And right doth never go forth;
> For the wicked doth beset the righteous;
> Therefore right goeth forth perverted.
>
> (Habukkuk 1:1–4)

Yet despite the harshness of this tirade, Habakkuk contends that
the victory of the wicked is only temporary; his advice is to be
strong in faith, for right will always overcome evil in the end.
    Another example, not less impressive, comes from the story of
Job, to which there are numerous allusions in *The Slave*:

> As God liveth, who hath taken away my right;
> And the Almighty, who hath dealt bitterly with me;
> All the while my breath is in me,
> And the spirit of God is in my nostrils,
> Surely my lips shall not speak unrighteousness,
> Neither shall my tongue utter deceit;
> Far be it from me that I should justify you;
> Till I die I will not put away my integrity from me,
> My righteousness I hold fast, and will not let it go;
> My heart shall not reproach me so long as I live.
>
> (Job 27:2–6)

The sentiments expressed by Habakkuk and Job clearly resound
in Jacob's own inner dialogue with God: "'I have no doubt that
you are the Almighty and whatever you do is for the best, but it

is impossible to obey the Commandment, Thou Shalt Love Thy God. No, I cannot, Father, not in this life'" (p. 108).

And yet, though his beliefs occasionally falter, "Jacob had refused to forsake the Jewish faith" (p. 5). He interprets his present condition and the experiences both he and the Jewish people have had in the global context of biblical time and history. He sees that the present suffering does not differ from that of his ancestors. He consoles himself by recalling the constant tribulations in the history of the Jews, when, at times, God hid his face and let his people be cruelly persecuted. But even at such times, the Almighty, as Jacob puts it, "continued to superintend the world" (p. 8), and the evil times were invariably succeeded by periods of abundance and joy.

The second danger to Jacob's survival is Wanda, with whom he falls passionately in love. He suspects that this affair will lead him astray and bring about his destruction. True, she is different from the rest of her countrymen; true, her language is on a much higher level than theirs; true, she saved his life on different occasions; true, she helped him to remain a Jew and perform his obligations. But, nevertheless, she is the forbidden fruit, a woman of another origin, one who does not know the truth. It is, therefore, in connection with Wanda that Singer creates one of the most elaborately structured paradoxes in his novel. The development of Jacob and Wanda's relationship turns into a process that leads to the affirmation of the Jewish faith, that makes Jacob a firmer believer in God's justice and mercy. Wanda, in her turn, joins the Jewish faith not only because of love, but, most important, because she believes in Jacob's convictions. While going through her conversion and becoming Sarah she becomes an art object, created by Jacob. Jacob carves her new identity in the same way that he carves the Ten Commandments in the rock. He molds her into a new being. At times, he feels guilty, but the rewards his liaison with Wanda offers him are enough to obliterate these feelings of discomfort. Singer structures the relationship between the Jewish man and the gentile woman according to the principles of the Bible itself: "And the Lord said, 'It is not good that man should be alone.'" Singer moves his characters toward communication and mutual understanding, the two components in the relationship between man and woman that help alleviate loneliness and yield satisfaction and joy.

The beginning of Wanda's conversion and Jacob's submission to sexual desires marks the end of his exile among the Polish peasants. Jacob's artful recreation of the past through the language he manages to preserve and his establishment of a monument to the Jewish faith by inscribing the Laws of Torah on a stone become the means of his physical and intellectual survival. Art, in short, helps him to transcend the hardships of exile. And it is not by chance that delivery from his first bondage comes through artists of sorts, that is, through circus actors who manage to convey Jacob's message to his countrymen. Again, we see how art and religion intersect and merge in Singer's novel. In addition, Jacob's delivery from captivity coincides with his discovery of yet another aspect of Judaism, which had to do with the relationship between man and man, rather than man and God.

When in captivity among the heathen villagers, Jacob became a full-fledged artist, who by erecting a monument to the Jewish faith restored his covenant with God. But this art object is only part of his overall artistic design; Wanda is the second half of it. Leaving her behind meant leaving behind part of himself and becoming susceptible to another kind of slavery. Jacob becomes a slave to his passion for the woman who under his influence went through tremendous changes and was left in exile among her own people. She comes close to a total acceptance of Judaism; with Jacob's help, her language improves to such an extent that it becomes a barrier between Wanda and her family; she becomes Jacob's faithful partner and companion as he is on his way to recognizing the often inexplicable ways of the Almighty. But most important, she now shares a common past with her Jewish lover. To leave her behind means not only betrayal of the art work that he initiates, but an almost certain death sentence for the woman who had turned into a total stranger among her own countrymen.

When Jacob is ransomed and comes home to Josefov, his worst suspicions are confirmed. His entire family has perished at the hands of Chmielnicki's murderers. Many of the survivors around him appear to be mentally crippled and impaired. The majority of his fellow Jews behave as if nothing happened, as if the recent events were a well-forgotten past. This is unbearable to Jacob, and "the best he could do is to stop thinking and desiring" (p.

89), when confronted with the unethical behavior of the people he idealized during the five years of his Polish exile. "The years of slavery," Singer comments, "had estranged him from life; he looked healthy but shattered within" (p. 119).

Furthermore, Jacob cannot understand the discrepancy in the everyday life of his countrymen. They observe every commandment in regard to God, but when dealing with each other they defile without hesitation the commandment to love their neighbor as they love themselves. To preserve his faith in Judaism, Jacob has to flee again. He has to go back to Wanda, with whom he can build a relationship that will restore and reaffirm his conviction in the possibility of obeying the words of God in regard to men as well. This is a heroic and often burdensome undertaking. "The day Jacob had left Josefov for the village where he had been a slave for five years, he had picked up a burden which became heavier with the passage of time. His years of enforced slavery had been succeeded by a slavery that would last as long as he lived" (p. 159).

Jacob finds Wanda in a dreadful mental state. He immediately understands that had he delayed his return any longer, she would have died. He also notices that the results of his teachings are nearly gone. Had Wanda perished, Jacob's overall artistic design, of which she was a significant part, would have never been completed.

Reunited again, Wanda-Sarah and Jacob after a long and dangerous journey arrive in Pilitz, a Jewish community established by the survivors of Chmielnicki's pograms. Sarah, instructed by Jacob, pretends to be a deaf mute. Although she speaks Yiddish well, her pronunciation would betray her gentile origins. If the community learns about Jacob's cohabitation with a Gentile woman not properly converted, he will be excommunicated. The laws of the Poles are even more cruel: Wanda faces certain death for abandoning her religion and converting to Judaism. The two enter now an existence of tightrope walkers; any slip on their part means inevitable disaster.

As I have pointed out earlier, Wanda-Sarah, by being an exile in Pilitz, must go through the same difficulties that Jacob endured in his exile among her countrymen. In his description of the Pilitz community, Singer draws almost an identical parallel between Pilitz and Wanda's village. Hypocrisy, slander, envy, and gossip are everyday occurrences here. Men forget past disasters too soon. They seem to be unaware that Judaism is not only about men's relationship to God but also about one's relationship to fellow men. The attitude the Pilitz Jews take toward Wanda-Sarah is much the same as the villagers took toward Jacob. There is also a conspicuous similarity between Gershon, the head of the Pilitz community, and Zagajek, the bailiff of the village.

Despite the difficulties Jacob and Wanda-Sarah have to endure, their situation is nevertheless different. They have a common experience—both Jacob and Sarah are strangers who live under the constant threat of being discovered. They share a common past; they can fully identify with each other. Furthermore, by educating Wanda and teaching her the language, by conversing about God and faith, Jacob is completing the second part of his artistic creation. Wanda-Sarah emerges under the loving hands of her creator as the perfect embodiment of a Jewish woman, an equal partner to her artist-husband. Her eagerness to learn is limitless; her ability to forgive and forget the wrongdoings of her neighbors is praiseworthy; her devotion to and oneness with Jacob are enviable. Wanda's pregnancy seals the integral unity of the couple. She will soon give birth to a baby in whom the strivings of both husband and wife to be faithful to God and kind to men will miraculously merge. The baby is to be, according to Singer's design, the crowning of Jacob's artistic endeavors.

The Pilitz exile has a tragic end for Sarah and Jacob—she dies in childbirth, while he is excommunicated by the Pilitz Jewish community and then arrested by government officials. Two details that have far-reaching consequences mark Singer's authorial design at this point. First, the baby boy survives; and, second, Jacob finally understands fully the meaning of the prayer, "Thou hast not made me a slave." When chained to the saddles of two horseback riders who are dragging him to town to face trial, it suddenly occurs to Jacob that chains can sometimes be broken. Nowhere is it written that a man has to consent to his own destruction. His mood changes; he becomes angry; he feels the awakening of new passions and half-forgotten desires. The reader has the sensation that a new man is being born at this point. Jacob's rebirth parallels the birth of his son, Benjamin. Interestingly enough, the same prayer that was recited to make Wanda's delivery easier can be applied to Jacob as well: "The captive exile hasteneth that he may be loosed and that he should not die in the pit" (p. 223). Aware now of his new identity, he knows exactly what to do. Like his biblical ancestor, Samson, Jacob violently tears apart the heavy chains, the chains that keep him fastened to his former existence, and flees toward freedom and a new life. He had thus, Singer comments, "outwitted the powerful, broken the chain of slavery" (pp. 251–52).

The author's intentions are clear. He associates Jacob's rebellion against slavery and exile with the call to the Jewish people to stand up to their oppressors and fight for their right to live in dignity, even though such a resolution may require sacrifices. They should no longer go to their graves like meek sheep. Resistance and armed struggle are seen as justifiable by present conditions. The need for energetic action against oppression and bigotry was recognized and sanctified by many Yiddish writers. "Bontsha the Silent," a masterful short story by I. L. Peretz (1851–1915), condemns meekness and submission and calls on Bontsha not to be silent anymore. The resolutions of the story and novel, however, are different. Peretz, in a tongue-in-cheek manner, sends his protagonist to heaven to be rewarded for his meekness;[13] Singer, in his turn, finds a better place for Jacob. He chooses the Holy Land as the only locale where his hero might obtain rest and fulfillment. And it is to the land of Israel that Jacob is duly sent.

Yet, Jacob cannot leave immediately; he must still perform another duty. At the end of the passage that related Jacob's shaking off the chains of slavery, Singer inserts a magnificent metaphor, embodied in the image of the protagonist's newborn son, that foreshadows the course of events not only of Jacob's life but also of his people. "At the edge of the horizon to his left a forest stretched like a sash of blue, and emerging from it like the head of a new-born child, small and bloody-red, came the sun" (p. 252). There are new horizons for Jacob and revived hopes in his existence. The description of the sun indicates both light and the bloody struggle that awaits his new awareness and his newborn baby. Looking at this sun, Jacob fully comprehends his obligations. Disregarding the mortal dangers of his return to Pilitz, he hastens back to recover Benjamin from the family that temporarily sheltered the child.

Jacob knows that carrying the boy away may mean subjecting him to death. And yet, he cannot be passive anymore. He has to act not only for his own sake, but also for the sake of Wanda-Sarah's memory, for the sake of the bond, their son, that keeps the living and the dead in a covenantal relationship. Benjamin becomes the symbol of the art that Jacob created, first by himself and then in a close partnership with Sarah. The baby is a *tabula rasa* on which the full text of the merger between faith and art will be written. The son of Jacob and Sarah's sorrows, their work of purity and perfection, is carried by Jacob to the one place where there should be no discrepancy between the relationship of man to God and that of man to man: that is, the Holy Land. There there is neither slavery nor exile, only hard work and the study of the Torah.

Exile, Singer implies, inevitably leads to death. Jacob spends twenty years in the Holy Land, working hard, helping the needy, watching his son become an instructor in a yeshiva, thus carrying on the tradition of his father. But as soon as he returns to Poland, his strength abates; he feels exhausted and finally dies without fulfilling his mission to retrieve Sarah's bones and have them buried next to his own grave on the Mount of Olives. Furthermore, exile also means a split in one's identity, which is best illustrated through language. It is not coincidental, therefore, that Singer's descriptions of the death of Jacob and Sarah are nearly identical. On her deathbed, "Sarah spoke a mixture of Polish and Yiddish" (p. 225); when Jacob is dying, "single words of Yiddish and Polish bubble from his throat" (p. 308). Benjamin will have only one language, one people, one identity.

There are means to transcend the state of transplantation and survive, but these apply only to individual characters, those of Nabokov and Conrad, for example. For Singer, the only way for an entire transplanted nation to survive is to recover its own land, with its language, laws and art—the basic elements of a new and liberated identity.

ENEMIES, A LOVE STORY

> *I have set before thee life and death, the blessing and the curse. Choose life that you may live.*
> Deuteronomy 30: 19

> *Auschwitz is modern civilization's declaration of bankruptcy.*
> Alexander Donat, *Jewish Resistance*

Since the end of World War II, writers of many kinds have been troubled by the question whether it is possible to find the proper form and the right diction to convey and recapture the enormity of evil that befell mankind in this century. Lionel Trilling contends that there are no adequate means or possible ways to communicate the incommunicable suffering of both the victims and the survivors,[14] that literature is doomed to fail when confronting the Holocaust. One can understand the concern and the despair of a man, himself a writer and literary critic, when only a few years after the Holocaust he feels helpless and resigned. Yet the question of adequacy is not adequate in this context; what is of utmost importance is to confront the experiences, no matter how atrocious. Silence, in this case, is a self-defeating means to make a point. When dealing with the Holocaust, Edward Alexander argues, "some degree of failure or inadequacy is almost a precondition of success in which we can expect no more than a shattered majesty and a noble imperfection."[15]

Writers on the whole did not shrink from their duty to depict the events of World War II. Many books in different genres of imaginative fiction have been written. Some failed, some succeeded. Yet all have added dimensions to the reader's awareness and understanding of the Holocaust. There are a few works that should never have been written, especially those mythologizing Hitler. Good literature, though, has far surpassed the trash that is its constant companion. Authors of the highest caliber felt that they had no right to circumvent Holocaust experiences; their task, therefore, was to face them with courage and the sense of performing a holy deed, owed both to the living and to the dead.

Elie Wiesel, Alexander Donat, Andre Schwartz-Bart, Piotr Rawicz, Abba Kovner, Haim Gouri, Susan Schaeffer, Jacob Glatstein, and Nelly Sachs are but a few who deal with the destruction of the Jews. Not all of these writers were survivors, but their license to address the subject is nonetheless valid. The reader will rarely find "answers" in their novels and poems. Most of these artists pose questions rather than render solutions; they state facts, make their characters think aloud, raise controversies. Their success lies in the new awareness they bring to the reader; their failure to supply a happy ending cannot be held against them. The literature of genocide is the literature of exclamation and question marks.

One of the writers who deals with the Holocaust is I. B. Singer. There is hardly a novel by Singer that does not, directly or indirectly, reflect the fate of Eastern European Jewry in the twentieth century. Singer was fortunate enough to have left Poland for the United States prior to the Nazi invasion in September 1939. His clear vision of what was to happen to his people in the nearest future led to his timely departure. He did not share his friends' views that the approaching catastrophe would somehow pass them. Unfortunately, most of the Polish Jews perished either in Nazi concentration camps and death factories or died in Siberia and Kazachstan, unable to endure the hardships of forced labor. Among the victims were Singer's professional colleagues as well as members of his immediate family. His mother, Bathsheva, and his brother, Moyshe, were not among the living when the war ended.

At the time of his emigration from Poland, Singer's artistic credibility rested on one novel only, *Satan in Goray.* Leaving behind him a potential audience of over three million speakers of Yiddish, he nevertheless had high hopes of launching a successful career in America. Upon arrival, though, the young artist was struck by a disease familiar to most exiled intellectuals, creative paralysis. The most obvious symptoms of this illness are the inability to compose, the failure to make contacts with a new audience, and a weakened confidence in one's native language. There were ample reasons for Singer's silence. As a displaced person, he experienced the many difficulties in adjustment and adᵔptation to the new circumstances an exiled state creates. An intellectual who wanted to survive as an artist, and, at the same time, preserve his own identity, Singer did not fail to perceive that Yiddish was declining and that Hebrew, after being revived in Palestine, was becoming a preferable medium of expression for a Jewish writer. Furthermore, numerous accounts of the Nazi atrocities were reaching the young writer. Their effect on Singer was twofold; he became deeply depressed by all that he heard; on the other hand, he felt guilty for abandoning his people in time of danger. Singer's state of spiritual paralysis lasted for eight years. Only in 1943 did he regain his creative powers and become a regularly published writer in *Der Forverts*, a New York–based Yiddish newspaper.

Despite his pessimistic views concerning the fate of Yiddish, Singer nevertheless chose to write in his native tongue and not to make the shift to English, though he had grown to have a good command of it. The subject matter of the majority of his novels and stories is the destiny of Eastern European Jewry as well as the lives of Holocaust survivors, a fact that greatly influenced his decision to compose in his mother tongue. Had he made up his mind to turn to English as a medium of artistic expression, he would have betrayed the memory of millions of Yiddish speakers who did not live to read his work. As for the survivors, their present lives could never be divorced from their past experiences, of which Yiddish was a crucial element. To create works about wartime and survivors means to compose in the survivors' language and to speak in their diction. Writing in Yiddish is for Singer a point of morality and ethics.

Singer, by his own admission, always writes about what he knows best. He knows best the Jewish milieu of prewar Poland; he knows best the Jewish milieu of the survivors, the displaced Jews from different European countries; these are his subjects. The souls of the victims and the ghosts of the survivors populate most of his books. Whenever Singer writes about prewar Poland, the reader must be conscious that Singer is describing a brutally destroyed world and that his composition is underscored by his knowledge of the deterioration of European civilization in the twentieth century. His writing about a vanished community is his tribute to the dead; his writing about the survivors is his duty to the living.

In his novel, *Enemies, A Love Story*, Singer writes about survivors in America; yet he constantly blurs the distinction between their prewar past and their exiled present. These are people who managed to go through the Nazi hell and who felt at the time of their liberation that they had no business in the countries of their birth. There were also those who went back to their villages and towns in Hungary, Czechoslovakia, Romania, Poland, and Germany, occupied now by Russians, with the hope of discovering a surviving relative. Many of them were trapped there; a few lucky ones succeeded in recrossing the border, seeking their fortunes elsewhere. Most of the survivors, rather than stay in Europe's Western democracies, set out in two directions, to Palestine, the land of their forefathers, and to America, the country of mythical opportunities. Unfortunately, they were not welcome in either of these places. The British who held the mandate over Palestine at the time were reluctant to resettle the survivors for political reasons. Neither was the United States swift in granting entry visas to the remnants of the European Jewry. Thousands of survivors were for years kept in the displaced persons' camps prior to acceptance by America. Nevertheless, these temporary delays and artificially imposed obstacles could not prevent most of them from finally settling in the country of their choice. This, then, is the background of most of Singer's characters in *Enemies, A Love Story*.

Many of Singer's major figures perceive themselves as walking corpses or as the souls of the dead. Frequently they think that being physically alive is not a joy but, rather, punishment. And although they are physically in America, mentally they are always looking backward toward past experiences, toward a world that keeps captive their true souls, which hover over the graves of their children, parents, and grandparents. Their current actions are the results of the forces of inertia; they are mechanical and their habits reflect past modes of life; they are void of true passions and emotions. No matter how hard these survivor-characters try to begin anew, to shake off the bad dreams, to rid themselves of the shadow of the past, they usually fail. Their emotions of loneliness, frustration, despair, and anger limit and paralyze them. Their exile, stripped of the spiritual values that are no longer relevant, evolves into a slow process of dying. Their losses are so overwhelming and haunting that even the rare moments of joy and forgetfulness they sometimes experience turn later into feelings of guilt for yielding to the pressures of everyday life and giving in to natural human instincts.

Enemies, A Love Story, is not Singer's first attempt to render the tragic situation of Jewish exiles in America. It is important to remember that their displacement assumes additional dimension by the fact that these exiles are Holocaust survivors. Numerous accounts of their, in most cases, tragic destinies, scattered in the writer's six compilations of stories published prior to the novel, make up the basis of his larger canvas. Thematically, the stories can be divided into two groups: those dealing with prewar Poland and those relating postwar experiences. The latter should be seen as the continuation of the former. Since, as I have mentioned earlier, the present lives of the survivors cannot be divorced from their past prewar experiences, the two groups of stories should be regarded as a continuous series in which each element depends on and complements the other. The novel incorporates and synthesizes the experiences related in the shorter pieces; it turns, thus, into an all-embracing study of different strata of Jewish population. Almost invariably, the setting is either New York's East Side or the villages and towns of prewar Poland. Herman Broder and the rest of the novel's major characters have their counterparts in such short stories as "Something Is There," "The Cafeteria," "The Safe Deposit," "The Cabbalist of East Broadway," and "The Key," to name just a few.

Herman Broder shares many similarities, both in his conduct and fate, with Rabbi Nechemia from Bechev in "Something Is There."[16] This spiritual leader of a rural Jewish community suddenly becomes aware that he cannot comply with the canons of Jewish teaching anymore. As a result, he divests himself of the responsibilities he has both to God and his people, and leaves for Warsaw in search of worldliness, enlightenment, and new meanings in life. The rabbi's journey in the city, which in Singer's description becomes an incarnation of evil, can be compared to an odyssey in Dante's *Inferno*. Nechemia's long-cherished joys of adventure do not materialize; the city is disappointing and offers nothing but sinful temptation. Ashamed of his weakness and his submission to Satan's will, he finally returns to Bechev. The ending of the story is ambiguous. It is not clear whether he assumes anew his rabbinic duties; yet, he now understands that being away from one's roots and traditions invariably leads to sin, assimilation, suffering, and even death. Herman Broder faces the same choices, but, unfortunately, there is no Bechev for him to return to.

Although another character, Professor Eibesschutz in "Pigeons," has devoted his entire life to the study of world history, he understands its full meaning only on his deathbed. While feeding pigeons, Professor Eibesschutz is physically assaulted by Polish anti-Semites. The wound they inflict is fatal to the scholar. During the last minutes of his life he summarizes all his knowledge: "it is the wicked who make history."[17] There is nothing left for him to do but quietly depart to other spheres, where the peaceful pastime of feeding pigions will not be disrupted by the wicked. Herman Broder, as we shall see, wholeheartedly embraces the professor's view.

Singer, as his memoirs testify, has always had an interest in philosophy. It is not surprising, then, that Herman Broder, the main protagonist of *Enemies, A Love Story* and in many ways the writer's mouthpiece, is a student of philosophy. Many intellectuals Singer describes in his short stories are philosophy students. Their views on the subject are basically those of Herman and of Singer as well. The surrealistic setting and the sombre atomosphere of "The Safe Deposit"[18] are appropriate to its phantasmagoric events and surprising conclusions. The tragic end of Uri Zalkind, a prominent professor of philosophy, is heightened by his heartbreaking realization that philosophy after the Holocaust is in a state of bankruptcy. It can explain nothing; it can help nobody. The results of Zalkind's lifelong research and reading are nothing more than an empty nutshell. Everything around him is meaningless and void of reason. These conclusions are reconfirmed by yet another philosopher, Joil Yabloner (in "The Cabbalist of East Broadway"),[19] who, like Professor Zalkind, finds no solace in the science to which he has devoted his whole life. His destiny is to become a permanent fixture in an anonymous cafeteria on East Broadway. Nothing can help him regain his belief in reason, the manmade idol of the enlightened philosophers.

As this brief survey suggests, Singer, long before writing *Ene-*

mies, A Love Story, had laid the groundwork for the novel in his numerous shorter pieces. His characters in the stories are divided into two groups: the victims and the survivors, the dead and the living. Reading the stories with a prewar setting, the reader is always aware that most characters are predestined to die; the stories with a postwar setting are usually populated by survivors whose perception of reality is incompatible with their experiences and the knowledge of the past. Singer's main interest lies in the understanding of the survivors who cannot "make it" in their new exile, that is, in America. The author tries to explore the reasons for their failure to lead a "normal life"; he wants to penetrate the mechanism of their self-destructive impulses. Finally, he makes us realize that exile for these people is synonomous with death, the latter being only chronologically postponed by their chance survival. Enemies, A Love Story, like Shosha and The Slave, does suggest ways to transcend exile and survive.

Singer's Holocaust exiles are complicated people, and to deal with them is not an easy task, nor one that can be pursued with emotional detachment. These characters are constantly posing questions although they know in advance what the answers are or rather, what their answers are. They have a strong, almost heroic urge to live, yet they are convinced, on the basis of their past experiences, of life's worthlessness. Furthermore, they are constantly fighting back the overwhelming natural instinct to multiply, that is, to start all over again. The violent repression of this desire is explained by a cold logic—they will not produce fuel for death camp chimneys. One moment the survivors will vehemently deny the existence of God, who looked the other way[20] while Jewish children were slaughtered, and the next they will reverently bow their heads before the Almighty in admission of the inexplicability of His ways. The dichotomy in their personalities is aggravated by the self-defeating inability to reconcile the longing to lead a "normal life" with the acute awareness that all that was holy to them is buried under ashes. Philosophy, history, religion, once the foundation of their existence, turn into empty words that do not make sense in the aftermath of the Holocaust. In short, these are people who have been made to exchange one exile for another, with all the miseries such a cruel displacement brings.

Singer's novel, a case study of Holocaust survivors' exile, makes clear the substantial difference between Polish exile and exile in America. As I have mentioned elsewhere, Jews lived in Poland for over eight hundred years, and during this time they succeeded, despite frequent massacres and persecutions, in building a coherent community and major centers of learning. The homogeneity of their social structure was threatened, to a large extent, by the advance of the Enlightenment in the nineteenth and the first quarter of the twentieth centuries. Assimilationist tendencies grew strong and could hardly have been contained even if Hitler had not existed. It is impossible to predict what would have become of the Polish Jewish community had it been left in peace, but chances are it would have gradually given in to the forces of worldliness and Enlightenment, thus bringing upon itself its own spiritual dissolution. The Holocaust has proven that whether or not one abandons the Jewish faith one is, nevertheless, bound by the collective destiny of his people. In *Enemies, A Love Story*, Singer implies that this cynical lesson has not yet been learned by the Jews in America.

The American Jewish community is relatively young. Eastern Europe has long been its main source of spiritual values and liveliness. The first Jewish settlers from Eastern Europe came to the United States as a result of political upheavals and pogroms. But in later years most of the emigrants were drawn to the United States for economic rather than political reasons. Among these were many, as Howe points out, who had positive aspirations toward a new life.[21] The American Jewish community, Singer suggests in a number of his stories and particularly in *Enemies, A Love Story*, was unprepared for the breed of exiles that began arriving after World War II. They wanted to see the survivors melt into the landscape as soon as possible, to forget about the terrible ordeal they had just gone through. By helping these people adapt to their new circumstances, the American Jews were in part trying to appease their own guilty consciences for not having done enough to help their brethren through the war years.

Singer's description of American Jews is not a flattering one. He seems irritated by their inability to see beyond the surface, to understand that the survivor-exile they are dealing with is a different type of exile, to perceive the deep psychological traumas

this exile suffers. Rabbi Lampert, Herman Broder's employer, is
a representative character in this respect. He is constantly scold-
ing Herman for being secretive, for not releasing his phone number, for not opening up. It is beyond his comprehension that the
money he pays Herman will not make up for the losses of this
man. "I want us to be friends," he tells Herman on one occasion,
"but there is something about you that makes it difficult. I could
help you a great deal, but you shut yourself up like an oyster.
What secrets are you hiding behind those proverbial seven
locks?"²² When Herman, after some hesitation, replies that "anyone who's gone through all that I have is no longer a part of this
world," Rabbi Lampert lashes out at him in a long and angry
tirade. He calls Herman's reply a cliché, "empty words." The
only thing the rabbi seems to be able to do is oppose Herman's
knowledge of deep human suffering with his superficial concep-
tion of man's nature:

> You are as much a part of this world as the rest of us. You
> may have been a step away from death a thousand times,
> but so long as you are alive and eat and walk, and, pardon
> me, go to the toilet, then you're flesh and blood like every-
> one else. I know hundreds of concentration camp sur-
> vivors, some of them were practically on the way to the
> oven—they are right here in America, they drive cars,
> they do business. Either you are in the other world or you
> are in this world. You can't stand with one foot on the
> ground and the other in the sky. You are playing a role,
> that's all. But why? (p. 25)

Needless to say, Rabbi Lampert does not get an answer from
Herman; neither does Herman release his phone number to him.
These two diametrically different men do not occupy the same
plane of existence. Herman belongs to the "half of his people"
who "had been tortured and murdered." And while this was happening, Rabbi Lampert was with the other half, "giving parties"
(pp. 213–14). There is no way, indeed, for the two to find a common language. Neither does the younger generation of American
Jews escape Singer's biting satire. He describes an episode in an

upstate New York resort in which a Holocaust survivor is brutally insulted by a mindless and cynical waiter. "One woman, a recent arrival in America, sent back her serving and the waiter asked 'By Hitler you ate better?'" (p. 120). After such episodes, how could anyone follow the rabbi's appeal "to open up"?

Rabbi Lampert's call to completely forget the past is brushed aside by Herman, who believes the past should be remembered; without it one cannot understand his present state, cannot retain the real identity of a Jew. Those who forget commit an outright sin against the victims as well as against the history of the Jewish people. Forgetfulness is synonymous with assimilation. Herman is simply not able to perceive how people, especially those who went through the Holocaust, can go on living as if nothing happened. When observing such survivors, "the broadbacked men and pretty women," whose talk is invariably centered around real estate and the stock market, Herman poses questions that are crucial for his survival of exile in America. "'In what way are they my brothers and sisters?'" Herman asked himself. "'What does their Jewishness consist of? What is my Jewishness?' They all had the same wish: to assimilate as quickly as possible and get rid of their accents. He belonged neither to them nor to the American, Polish, or Russian Jews." (p. 114). This passage defines four problems that Herman faces: the past, the Jewishness of his people, his own identity, and his true home. If, in the course of the novel, he can resolve the four problems, his survival will be assured. If he fails, there is no hope that he may transcend exile.

An intellectual and an artist of sorts, in Poland Herman Broder wrote a dissertation dealing with worldly philosophy. This, however, did not prevent him from being well versed in Talmudic scholarship. Shortly after marrying Tamara and fathering two children, Herman concluded that family life did not suit him. After all, he was a faithful student of Schopenhauer. The war made irreversible his separation from his daughter and son; he never saw them again. Because of the kindness of Yadwiga, a Polish servant girl in his parents' house, Herman survived the Holocaust. She hid him in a hayloft for three long years, becoming in the meantime both his mistress and savior. Grateful to Yadwiga for unfaltering devotion, Herman, after having witnesses confirm the death of his children and wife, married her and brought her over to America. Yet prior to coming to the United States, the two had to wait for over a year in a German displaced persons' camp for their entry visas. In Germany Herman meets Masha, the woman who will become his mistress and cause his downfall.

Once in the United States, Herman starts to earn his living as a teacher of Talmud. This, however, does not satisfy his intellectual urges to create. Yet the closest he comes to any kind of creative work is through Rabbi Lampert, who employs him as a ghostwriter. Herman despises his job, but he carries it out to the best of his abilities. It allows him, after all, to make a living as well as to be in close proximity to the written word.

Yadwiga, in the meantime, takes care of the household chores, learns to be Jewish, and cherishes the rare moments she can be with her husband. To spend time with Masha, Herman invents lies that keep him away from home for many days in a row. He assures Yadwiga that he is selling books and therefore must travel frequently. Herman constantly fears being exposed and reported for his misconduct. Yet Masha, his only genuine love and passion, in his view repays the risk.

As if this situation were not complicated enough, Herman suddenly learns about his first wife's resurrection from the dead: she was only wounded by the bullet that supposedly killed her, and, under the cover of night, she managed to crawl through the heaps of dead human bodies to seek refuge in a nearby village. Tamara assures her husband that she holds no claims upon him and will grant him, if he wishes, a legal divorce. To confuse things still more, Herman, on the spur of the moment, gives in to Masha's exhortations to marry her, becoming thus the husband of three wives simultaneously.

Had the events in the novel not been caused by the Holocaust and had its characters not been Nazi survivors, the above synopsis of the plot could have easily served as an outline of a cheap Hollywood production. The novel, though, is a serious work of literature. It is hard to overlook its affinities and similarities with *Shosha* and *The Slave* in particular. *Enemies, A Love Story* is part of Singer's exploration of exile. In *Shosha*, as I pointed out earlier, Singer defines the writer, the intellectual, as a true representative of an exiled people who is assigned the duty of a rememberer and who becomes the only link that holds together the divergent strata of the Jewish people. The closest Singer comes to providing unambiguous and direct solutions of how to transcend exile and survive both physically and intellectually is in *The Slave*. In this novel, the writer defines the key elements needed to survive exile: language, intellect, tradition, and art. For the Jewish people, there exists yet another ingredient, that is, the return to the land of their fathers. Both *Shosha* and *The Slave* are accounts of triumph; *Enemies, A Love Story* is a study of failure.

If after reading *Enemies, A Love Story*, one were to return to the first paragraph of the novel (Singer starts and completes the book with the name Herman), he would notice that the introductory passage contains all the problems the work raises. Moreover, it foreshadows the ending of the novel:

> Herman Broder turned over and opened one eye. In his dreamy state, he wondered whether he was in America, in Tzivkev, or in a German camp. He even imagined himself hiding in a hayloft in Lipsk. Occasionally all of these places fused in his mind. He knew he was in Brooklyn, but he heard the Nazis shouting. They were jabbing him with their bayonets, trying to flush him out, while he pressed deeper and deeper into the hay. The blade of the bayonet touched his head.
>
> Full awakening required an act of volition. (p. 3)

Herman Broder, as we see, is not dead, yet neither is he fully alive; he is not asleep, yet he is not awake either. He dreams, but his dreams are a fusion of imaginary and real nightmares. Herman Broder is walking a thin line between life and death, present and past, reality and fantasy, truth and deception, art and pseudoart, and finally, Judaism and worldliness. Similar to the rest of the novel's major characters, he is a somnambulistic character. One careless step can cause his downfall.

Even before the second World War, Herman Broder was not exactly a happy man. His marriage failed—for an enlightened Jew and devotee of Schopenhauer, marriage was not a viable institution. Nationalism and religion were an anathema to him. Consequently, he became an exile among exiles, lonely, despised by his family, disregarded by the traditional Jews, sneered at by his fellow intellectuals.

The Holocaust adds another dimension to Herman's exile in America. His shield of cynicism, behind which he was hiding for a long time, is shattered. Against his own will he finds himself married three times. Nothing he believes in seems to be true anymore. History turns into a mockery of mankind's progress:

> The idle promises of progress were no more than a spit in the face of the martyrs of all generations. If time was just a form of perception, or a category of reason, the past is as present as today: Cain continues to murder Abel. Nebuchadnezzar is still slaughtering Zedekia and putting out Zedekia's eyes. The pogrom of Kishinev never ceases. Jews are forever being burned in Auschwitz. Those without courage to make an end to their existence have only one way out: to deaden their consciousness, choke their memory, extinguish the last vestige of hope. (p. 30)

Herman's ahistorical view of mankind's development is matched by his bitter frustration and disappointment in philosophy, the science that only a few years previously had been revered and idolized by him:

> What could save Herman from sinking even deeper into the mire in which he was caught? Not philosophy, not Berkeley, Hume, Spinoza, not Leibnitz, Hegel, Schopenhauer, Nietzsche, or Husserl. They all preached some sort of morality but it did not have the power to help withstand temptation. One could be a Spinozaist and a Nazi; one could be versed in Hegel's phenomenology and be a Stalinist; one could believe in monads, in the Zeitgeist, in blind will, in European culture, and still commit atrocities. (p. 170)

Both in *Shosha* and in *The Slave*, Singer suggests that writing and visual art can serve as a means to transcend exile. Aaron Greidinger brings together different groups of Jews with the help of his art. Jacob constantly works on his art project; he sees in it the only way to salvation. Art is also one of the options that

Singer offers to Herman, but Herman abuses it. Even while hiding in the hayloft in Poland he make notes, trying to create something to keep him going, to help him survive. He is always putting pen to paper, working on his calligraphy, drawing pictures. But the results of his artwork are grotesque, to say the least. "He drew pictures of outlandish creatures with protruding ears, long beaks, and round eyes, and surrounded them with trumpets, horns, and adders. He even wrote in his dreams—on yellowish paper in Rashi script, a combination of a story book, cabalistic revelations and scientific discoveries" (p. 41). Herman's surrealistic pictures, which curiously resemble Chagall's drawings, as well as his writing in different genres and modes, reflect the state of mind of a man who constantly lives in a "presuicidal gloom." His art—no better than reality—does nothing to resolve his problems or ensure his survival. Rootless and detached, it generates despair rather than joy and beauty.

In America, Herman returns to his writing, though only as a ghostwriter, as Singer pointedly notes. Herman writes for Rabbi Lampert, doing a job rather than engaging in a creative process. A ghost, a somnambulist, an apparition, he carries out all his activities as if in a daze, though he refuses to submit to total destruction. He tries to see the rationale behind his actions; yet when he finds it faulty he nevertheless goes on performing these actions. His incessant activity becomes a means of fending off dark and misanthropic thoughts. Immersing himself in activities he knows to be purposeless, he can go on living without submitting to the suicidal urges that his thoughts and the reality around him generate. Even his three marriages are a fence behind which he is hiding, as if he were back in his Polish hayloft.

Very often amazed at Tamara's and Masha's behavior, Herman cannot understand why both women are so attracted to him, why they are taking care of him even though he has hardly brought any joy into their lives. "'What was it they all wanted?'" he asks on one occasion. His answer to his question applies not only to these two female survivors but to himself as well. They want, Herman says, "to forget for a while their loneliness and the inevitability of death" (p. 94), which is exactly what Herman desires. His tragedy is that he does not have a sense of belonging; he is uprooted, a branch cut off a tree.

In his recurrent and extreme states of despair, suicide appears the only logical way out of his misery. But, as Singer points out, he lacks the "courage to commit suicide," and all he can do is "shut his eyes, stop up his ears, close his mind, live like a worm" (p. 19). Singer's overall design, though, keeps Herman on the tightrope of existence for as long as it takes to explore all the options of survival.

One of the options he offers him is to father a child; by failing to do this, Herman yields a posthumous victory to Hitler, according to Emil L. Fackenheim, a prominent Jewish philsopher who calls on the Jews not to cooperate with Hitler, completing their destruction by refusing to multiply. In the aftermath of the Holocaust, such an attitude would mean "to respond to Hitler by doing his work."[23] Yet Herman's "greatest fear was his fear of again becoming a father. He was afraid of a son and more afraid of a daughter, who would be an even stronger affirmation of the positivism he rejected, the bondage that had no wish to be free, the blindness that wouldn't admit it was blind" (p. 149). Both Yadwiga and Masha, his two wives, beg him for a child; invariably he answers no. Yet despite his stubbornness, the gentile woman who converts to Judaism becomes pregnant and gives birth to a daughter. Life-giving forces transcend Herman's destructive impulses. One cannot turn his back, Singer implies, on faith and destiny. Even Masha, a walking monument to Nazi atrocities, the woman who embodies all the devastating effects of the Holocaust on the Jewish people, even she wants to become a mother. But Singer denies her this sacred right of womanhood. Her womb is barren; her pregnancy is a sham. Too similar to Herman, she contributes to his downfall. Masha is the claim of the past upon Herman..

As in other works by transplanted writers, the main characters must learn how to balance past and present and establish an equilibrium betweeen the two. If they live only in the past, they share the fate of Nabokov's Anton Sergeyevich Podtyagin or Sebastian Knight. Herman's dreams are as dark as those of the Russian poet; Masha is analogous to the Russian femme fatale who destroys Sebastian. Yet regardless of these two elements of destruction, Singer offers Herman another option to survive. If Herman accepts it, he can restore his identity as a Jew and can regain his sense of belonging. All he needs is to recognize that a Jew without Judaism is a nonentity.

At the beginning of the novel, Herman asks himself a question crucial to his existence: "How could his actions ever be explained to make sense? He had sinned against Judaism, American law, morality" (p. 23). Yet after acknowledging his misconduct, he proceeds in his old ways. Whenever life becomes unbearable to him, he invariably pledges to return to tradition and his faith. Herman clearly perceives the purpose of "modern" Judaism: "to ape the gentile." He sees modern Jews wearing skullcaps so small that they can hardly be seen. The diminishing size reflects their decreasing devotion to true Judaism. This for Herman signifies hypocrisy. These are not the people he would like to join. Drawn to the white-bearded sages, whom he sees through the window of a study house, poring over the yellow pages of scholarly works, Herman has a desire to join them, to become one with them; he intuitively feels that the truth flourishes with these stalwarts of traditional religion. Observing such people, Herman always arrives at the same conclusion: "if a Jew departed in as much as one step from the Shulcan Aruch, he found himself spiritually in the sphere of everything base—Fascism, Bolshevism, murder, adultery, drunkenness" (p. 170). Herman constantly castigates himself for not being able to stick to his resolutions to go back to the source: "How many times had he tried to spit in the face of worldliness, and each time been tricked away' (pp. 213–14).

When Tamara finally manages to bring some order into Herman's life, to reunite him with what he likes best, namely, books, a sudden fatal phone call shatters Herman's seemingly reordered life. The call is the call of the past that is irreconcilable with the present, the call that nullifies any possibilities of Herman's survival. Not even his dead father's voice, clearly heard by Herman in the midst of his chaotic existence, can be of any help to him: "'Well I ask you, what have you accomplished? You've made yourself and everyone else wretched. We are ashamed of you here in Heaven'" (p. 206). When Aaron Greidinger had a similar experience, he found the strength to run away from Betty, who, like Masha, had a destructive influence upon him. Not Herman: he joins Masha and all that she represents.

Herman's longing for Masha is easy to understand: she shares with him the same experiences; her dreams are identical to Herman's; her denial of God's existence in the aftermath of the Holocaust is more acceptable to him than the canons of Judaism. Anyone who penetrates the workings of Masha's mind can sympathize with her. "'I lie there,'" she once says, "'and remember all the savagery, all the humiliations. If I do sleep, then I am back with them immediately. They are dragging me, beating me, chasing me. They come running from all sides, like hounds after a hare'" (p. 95). Herman's thoughts coupled with those of Masha can generate only one outcome, the final one: death.

To counter the self-destructive elements among the Jews in this novel, Singer introduces two minor characters, Reb Abraham Nissen and his wife, who, despite what happened to the Jews, see one way only for their survival. "'When people stop believing in the Creator,'" Reb Nissen says, "'Anarchy prevails.'" He continues, "'The Torah says, 'For the imagination of man's heart is evil from his youth.' But that is why there is a Torah'" (p. 79). It is not surprising then, that the older couple finally find their peace only when they move to the land of their fathers. This is the way to true survival and transcendence of exile, when all other means are exhausted. Singer in his own way calls for the renewal of the covenant with God. The words of the theologian Abraham Joshua Heschel echo strongly through Singer's novel:

> The Almighty has not created the universe that we may have the opportunities to satisfy our greed, envy and ambition. We have not survived that we may waste our years in vulgar vanities. The martyrdom of millions demands that we consecrate ourselves to the fulfillment of God's dream of salvation.[24]

Singer's novel ends on a semioptimistic note. Herman vanishes, as is indeed foreshadowed at the beginning of the book; but Yadwiga, who calls herself the daughter of Israel, gives birth to a baby girl. She pointedly names her Masha. This name has a symbolic meaning: the very fact of the girl's birth is the affirmation of life; her name is a tribute to the Holocaust victims. The past and the present can coexist and be balanced; they do not exclude but complete each other.

Epilogue

Nor can one help the exile, the old man
Dying in a motel, with a loud fan
Revolving in the torrid prairie night
And, from the outside, bits of colored light
Reaching his bed like dark hands from the past
Offering gems; and death is coming fast.
He suffocates and conjures in two tongues
The nebulae dilating in his lungs.
Vladimir Nabokov, *Pale Fire*

Exile is a state of being that can never be fully grasped by an outsider, yet it is a phenomenon that fascinates many. People who are born into a free democratic society find it difficult to understand that there are still many countries in which the fate of the citizens is decided by the capricious whims of dictatorial leaders and by political intrigues directed primarily toward the suppression of individual freedoms and rights. Such countries are the main "producers" and "suppliers" of exiles.

History has witnessed numerous events, sometimes of enormous magnitude, that caused the displacement not only of individuals but of entire populations as well. The destinies of uprooted people are the subject matter of historical and sociological studies. These studies center on the transplanted intellectuals who, because of the nature of their vocations, face the severest difficulties when confronted with an exiled existence. Their hardships are mainly caused by detachment from the life-giving sources that fed their intellectual endeavors. Very often, however, the books about the transplants refer only to exiles

121

who earned their reputation in their homelands and who were forced, because of political circumstances, to flee from their native soil and find refuge in other countries. A prime example of this kind of study is the collection of essays *The Intellectual Migration*. Although it does not offer an in-depth research of exile and its consequences, the essays provide an abundance of names, statistical material, and references, as well as a comprehensive bibliography, all pertaining to the transplanted intellectuals of the nineteen thirties through the fifties. One group of intellectuals, that is, men of letters, is conspicuously left out. The reason for their absence, the editors explain, is the minimal contribution made by exiled writers to the intellectual life of their new countries.

A more serious approach to the problems of transplantation is attempted by H. Stuart Hughes in his excellent and ambitious book, *The Sea Changes*. The author, however, limits his scope mostly to philosophers, sociologists, historians, and psychoanalysts. The book can nevertheless serve as a model for a similar study of the life and work of transplanted writers. That there is need of such an undertaking is proven by the success of the symposia on exiled writers conducted in the pages of the *Saturday Review* and *Books Abroad* as early as 1940. The symposia attracted a wide range of responses both from well-known people and from individuals of different walks of life. A recent essay by Alfred Kazin, "The European Writers in Exile," testifies that the interest in intellectual transplantation is still lively. The reluctance of researchers to undertake serious studies of literary transplants is understandable, since this kind of transplantation is the most complicated and problematic. Yet through the lives and fiction of men of letters, we gain the most profound insight into exile and its essence.

In 1953, the University of Pennsylvania Press published a collection of five essays, *The Cultural Migration*. All reputable transplanted intellectuals of different vocations and divergent views, the contributors share an understanding of exile, aptly summarized by Franz Neuman, a famous sociologist who fled from Nazi anti-Semitism to America:

> If the intellectual has to give up his country, he does more than change his residence. He has to cut himself off from

an historical tradition, a common experience; has to learn
a new language; has to think and experience within and
through it; has, in short, to create a totally new life. It is
not the loss of a profession, of property, of status—that
alone and by itself is painful—but rather the weight of
another national culture to which he has to adjust
himself.[1]

In the same essay, Neuman refers to an article by G. G. Coulton,
"The Death Penalty for Heresy from 1184 to 1921 A.D.," that
traces the origin of the word *exile*. When the Romans and Greeks
banished rebellious intellectuals and artists, they used the term
extermination for this harsh punishment. In the third century
A.D. this term underwent substantial changes and assumed its
modern meaning: destruction.[2]

Neuman has identified a problem that any intellectual must
face after being banished from his native land. On the one hand,
the transplant is a bearer of past experiences; on the other, he
must cope with new realities, with a new present. His survival
depends on his ability to resolve this dichotomy in exiled existence. The sociologist's reference to Coulton's article points to
the fact that unless an equilibrium between past and present is
found, the transplant's fate is apt to be tragic and can end in destruction. Neuman's insight into the problems and destiny of intellectual exiles in general is applicable to literary transplants.

It is impossible to know whether or not Conrad, Nabokov, and
Singer were aware of the connotation of the word *exile* to which
Neuman refers; but as my study of the works and lives of these
authors shows, it becomes clear that the three share the view
that exile can indeed turn into a tragic and fatal experience. Despite Nabokov's small joke about his fiction being "Conradi-
cally" different from that of his Polish colleague, and regardless
of Singer's still smaller joke dismissing Nabokov because of the
latter's murderous attitudes toward innocent butterflies, I believe that these transplanted writers have more in common than
they care to admit. They sing themselves in their writing, to par-
aphrase Whitman's view of his relation to his art. One may argue
that every writer's fiction is to a certain degree autobiographical, but in the works of literary transplants this quality becomes
pervasive, unusually overt, and very often even obsessive. The

reason for this is simpler than it may seem. On the one hand, by fictionalizing their highly personal and private experiences, the transplanted writers lend shape to and give expression to problems that are close to them; they also enable the reader to understand the nuances of exiled existence and to gain a more profound insight into the workings of "transplanted minds." On the other hand, by reliving their own lives in their fictions, by making their characters share the burden of exile with them, they find it easier to transcend their own "unnatural state of existence." Because they constantly blend biography and fiction, Conrad, Nabokov, and Singer are often accused of being repetitous and circular. Repetitious and circular their subjects and characters may be; yet each of their novels and stories adds a new dimension to the reader's understanding of the problem of exile.

Conrad, Nabokov, and Singer are indeed prolific writers. As if afraid that something might stop their creative process, they are constantly on the run in their efforts to beat the clock. They are unwilling to plant roots in one place for a long time. They are aware that exile may mean death. But they do not fear physical destruction; it is, instead, spiritual death that frightens them. In their countries of exile the transplanted authors try everything possible to survive as artists. They understand that becoming "one of them"—melting into the landscape, obliterating individuality, adopting and fully adjusting to the new reality—means oblivion. This, they come to recognize, will cause the destruction of what is a major part of them—it will mean the denial of the source that feeds their creative imagination. On the other hand, Nabokov, Conrad, and Singer are aware of the dangers a stubborn clinging to the past may generate. Although they know that their past is always within them, that it cannot be ignored, they nevertheless seek consciously to preserve it. They try to achieve both in their personal lives and in their fiction the means of striking a balance between the "now" and the "then," between the "before" and the "after." Through their writing they find this desired equilibrium. Each new literary creation becomes a milestone on a path to survival.

Joseph Conrad, in his efforts to transcend exile and come to terms with his "unnatural state of existence," rightfully belongs to the literary subgenre I call transplanted authors. Though the circumstances of his life were different, the problems with which he had to cope were identical to those of Nabokov and Singer. Unlike his Russian and Yiddish colleagues, he never loosened his grip on his fictional characters. The Polish writer could not purge himself of the guilt he felt for betraying his native land. Regardless of his persistent attempts to "out-England England" he remained a Pole whose tragedy implied the inability to balance his deeply rooted nationalism and his natural longing for cosmopolitanism. Conrad survived his own exile; but for this survival his fictional doubles had to pay with their lives. He never gained the strength, the self-confidence, the firm ground of Nabokov and Singer. His art did not suffer from the lack of these qualities, however, even if the artist did.

Nabokov underwent several stages in order to transcend exile. Prior to writing in English, he created nine novels in his native language. Invariably his fictional characters suffer tragic fates. Most can never rid themselves of the burdens of the past; they collapse under this heavy load. Nabokov's shift to English reveals new intellectual strengths; it indicates his understanding that the wheel of history cannot be put in a reverse motion. He understands that the present cannot be ignored; it is not an illusion—it is real. This recognition makes him more tolerant both of his fictional characters and of himself. Past and present meet in his art, to which he builds a magnificent monument composed of his novels, stories, and poems.

Singer, for his part, experienced the same difficulties his Russian colleague had to cope with. His task of survival was more exhausting and burdensome because his subject was how both an individual character and a whole transplanted nation, the Jews of Poland, could transcend exile. Like his Russian counterpart, he becomes aware that exile can be synonymous with death; he also recognizes that art is indeed a means of survival for the transplanted writer. But he discovers, too, that for the Jewish nation to transcend its exile art will hardly be enough. It should be supplemented by faith, if not in religion then in peoplehood or nationality. The convergence of the two will secure not only the survival of an individual talent but the survival of the genius of a whole people.

Many of Singer's characters are survivors or victims of the Holocaust. The Yiddish writer commemorates their lives and deaths in Yiddish, a language that expresses their national identity, their mentality, the workings of their minds. The shift to English would, in Singer's view, betray the memory of the dead and fail to live up to the expectations of the survivors. A Jewish writer is seen by his people as a recorder and rememberer of their destinies, as one who makes them see that the Torah encompasses the relationship not only between man and God but between man and man as well. Singer never fails to live up to these expectations; and through this commitment he survives.

My study of these three exiled authors seeks to elucidate certain patterns common to their art and aspires to balance rather than exhaustiveness. It represents an initial stage in understanding the marginal existence of literary transplants.

Notes

CHAPTER ONE

1. Arthur Symons, *Notes on Joseph Conrad: With Some Unpublished Letters*, p. 18.

2. Conrad, Preface to *A Personal Record*, p. xv. Unless otherwise stated, the page numbers referring to the novels and stories of Joseph Conrad are those of the *Complete Works*.

3. Ibid., p. 95.

4. Gustav Morf, *The Polish Shades and Ghosts of Joseph Conrad*, p. 195.

5. Conrad, "The Secret Sharer," p. 132.

6. Conrad, "Heart of Darkness," p. 82.

7. Author's Note to *Youth*, p. xi.

8. A. T. Quiller-Couch, "Four Tales by Mr. Conrad," in *Conrad: The Critical Heritage*, p. 156.

9. See, for example, Thomas Moser, *Joseph Conrad: Achievement and Decline*, p. 267; Jocelyn Baines, *Joseph Conrad: A Critical Biography*, p. 267; Gustav Morf, *The Polish Heritage of Joseph Conrad*, pp. 168–69.

10. Richard Herndon, "The Genesis of Conrad's 'Amy Foster,'" p. 566.

11. Robert Andreach, "The Two Narrators of 'Amy Foster.'"

12. Conrad, "Amy Foster," p. 106. Subsequent references to this story will appear in the text.

13. Conrad, *Victory*, p. 217.

14. Frederick R. Karl, *Joseph Conrad: The Three Lives*, p. 513.

15. Conrad, *A Personal Record*, p. 122.
16. Ibid., p. 39.
17. Ibid., p. 136.
18. Conrad, *Notes on Life and Letters*, p. 155.
19. Conrad, Author's Note to *A Personal Record*, p. vii.
20. Leo Gurko, *Joseph Conrad: Giant in Exile*, p. 50.
21. Conrad, Author's Note to *A Personal Record*, p. viii.
22. Zdizislaw Najder, *Conrad's Polish Background: Letters to and from Polish Friends*, p. 180.
23. "Genesis," Herndon, pp. 560–61. This foreshadowing of Yanko's fate has been noticed by several critics.
24. Conrad, Author's Note to *Youth*, p. xi.
25. Ibid., p. x.
26. Conrad, "Heart of Darkness," p. 23. Subsequent references to this novel will appear in the text.
27. Stephen A. Reid, "The Unspeakable Rites," in *Conrad: A Collection of Critical Essays*, p. 45.
28. Morf, *The Polish Shades and Ghosts of Joseph Conrad*, pp. 150–51.
29. Conrad, "Autocracy and War," in *Notes on Life and Letters*, p. 100.
30. Conrad, *Under Western Eyes*, p. 288.
31. Jeffrey Berman, *Joseph Conrad: Writing as Rescue*, p. 132.
32. Jessie Conrad, *Joseph Conrad and His Circle*, p. 143.
33. Conrad, *Victory*, p. 217.
34. Ibid., p. 405.

CHAPTER 2

1. Ludmila A. Foster, "Nabokov in Russian Emigre Criticism," p. 43.
2. Vladimir Nabokov, *Mary*, p. 5. Subsequent references to this edition will appear in the text.
3. Andrew Field, *Nabokov: His Life in Art*, p. 126.
4. "Bluffs and Blindfolds—Nabokov's First Novel," *Times Literary Supplement*, 26 February 1971, p. 233. In 1971, in its February issue, *The Times Literary Supplement* attributed Field's error to a probable German mistranslation of the book; this was promptly refuted by Gleb Struve, a prominent Russian literary critic and a long-standing friend of Nabokov, who confirmed the mistake of his Australian colleague.
5. In his book *Vladimir Nabokov: America's Russian Novelist*, p. 41. It is surprising that G. M. Hyde calls this job "a favorite occupation of the Russian emigrés." Once proud and deeply rooted in their culture, language, and land, Russian exiles could only scoff and smile bitterly if they were told that being an extra was a "favorite occupation." Demeaning as it was, they had to do it because it was one of the jobs they could get.
6. This device of having a character walk into a novel or play one

moment and withdraw from it another without ever returning was, according to Nabokov, first used by Gogol. Twenty-two years after writing *Mary*, Nabokov in his book *Gogol*, a critical tribute of high esteem paid to the Russian genius, explains the significance of this technique which he himself is utilizing so skillfully in his own works.

7. Vladimir Nabokov, *Speak, Memory: An Autobiography Revisited*, p. 245.

8. Interview with Peter Duval-Smith and Christopher Burstall in Vladimir Nabokov, *Strong Opinions*, p. 12.

9. Interview with Alfred Appel, Jr., ibid., p. 78

10. Nabokov, *Nikolai Gogol*, p. 70.

11. L. L. Lee, *Vladimir Nabokov*, pp. 37–38.

12. Interview with Peter Duval-Smith and Christopher Burstall in Nabokov, *Strong Opinions*, p. 15.

13. Interview with Robert Hughes, ibid., p. 54.

14. Interview with Alfred Appel, Jr., ibid., pp. 88–89.

15. Vladimir Nabokov, "We So Firmly Believed," in *Poems and Problems*, p. 89. Subsequent references to this edition will appear in the text.

16. Interview with Allen Talmey, in *Strong Opinions*, p. 156.

17. John Hayman, "A Conversation with Vladimir Nabokov—with Digressions," p. 449.

18. Vladimir Nabokov, *The Real Life of Sebastian Knight*, p. 205. Subsequent references to this edition will appear in the text.

19. Simon Karlinski, ed. *The Nabokov–Wilson Letters*, p. 49.

20. Vladimir Nabokov, "Fame," in *Poems and Problems*, p. 103.

21. Interview with Peter Duval-Smith and Christopher Burstall in Nabokov, *Strong Opinions*, p. 18.

22. Interview with Alvin Toffler, ibid., p. 37.

23. Interview with Herbert Gold, ibid., p. 106.

24. Interview with Herbert Gold, ibid., p. 106.

25. Karlinski, *The Nabokov–Wilson Letters*, p. 50.

26. Ibid., p. 309.

27. Howard Nemerov, *Poetry and Fiction: Essays*, p. 261.

28. Charles Nicol, "Pnin's History," p. 198.

29. Interview with Alfred Appel, Jr., in *Strong Opinions*, p. 84.

30. Vladimir Nabokov, *Pnin*, pp. 19–20. Subsequent references to this edition will appear in the text.

31. H. Grabes, *Fictitious Biographies: Vladimir Nabokov's English Novels*, p. 46.

32. Aharon Appelfeld, "Badenheim 1939," p. 93.

33. Douglas Fowler, *Reading Nabokov*, p. 130.

34. Ambrose Gordon, Jr., "The Double Pnin," p. 152.

35. Interview with Alvin Toffler, in *Strong Opinions*, pp. 27–28.

CHAPTER 3

1. I. B. Singer, "The Lecture," in *The Seance and Other Stories*, p. 66. Subsequent references to this edition will appear in the text.

2. I. B. Singer, *Shosha*, p. 7. Subsequent references to this edition will appear in the text.

3. Edward Alexander, *Isaac Bashevis Singer*, p. 113.

4. The idea of an artist's omnipotence as a peacemaker in times of crises caused by exile has been explored by Singer on earlier occasions as well. The story "The Yearning Heifer" is typical in this respect. Only through the generous efforts of a Jewish writer is peace restored among the members of a troubled family, which finds itself transplanted to an isolated farm somewhere in New York State. A young writer's presence in their home makes the members of the family forget their troubles and cope with their exiled situation.

5. Alexander, *Isaac Bashevis Singer*, p. 73.

6. Ibid., p. 73.

7. Susan Sontag, "Demons and Dreams," p. 460.

8. Irving Malin, *Isaac Bashevis Singer*, pp. 58–59.

9. Frederick R. Karl, "Jacob Reborn, Zion Regained: I. B. Singer's *The Slave*," p. 122.

10. I. B. Singer, *The Slave*, p. 84. Subsequent references to this edition will appear in the text.

11. Paul Kresh, *Isaac Bashevis Singer: The Magician of West 86th Street*, p. 276.

12. Solo W. Baron, "Medieval Folklore and Jewish Fate," in *Jewish Heritage Reader*, p. 178.

13. I. L. Peretz, "Bontsha the Silent," in *The Heath Introduction to Fiction*, p. 161.

14. Lionel Trilling, "Art and Fortune," in *The Liberal Imagination*, pp. 264–65.

15. Edward Alexander, *The Resonance of Dust: Essays on Holocaust Literature and Jewish Fate*, p. xiii.

16. I. B. Singer, "Something Is There," in *A Friend of Kafka and Other Stories*, pp. 283–311.

17. I. B. Singer, "Pigeons," ibid., p. 120.

18. I. B. Singer, "The Safe Deposit," in *Old Love and Other Stories*, pp. 183–87.

19. I. B. Singer, "The Cabbalist of East Broadway," in *A Crown of Feathers*, p. 140.

20. One of Wiesenthal's characters expresses the same notion: "God was on leave" when the Nazi atrocities were happening. Simon Wiesenthal, *The Sunflower*, p. 13.

21. Irving Howe, *World of Our Fathers*.

22. I. B. Singer, *Enemies, A Love Story*, p. 25. Subsequent references to this edition will appear in the text.

23. Emil Fackenheim, "The Voice of Auschwitz," pp. 188–89.

24. Abraham Joshua Heschel, "The Meaning of This Hour," p. 492.

EPILOGUE

1. Franz L. Neuman, "The Social Sciences," p. 12.
2. Ibid., p. 7.

Bibliography

PRIMARY SOURCES

Joseph Conrad

"Amy Foster." *Complete Works*. 26 vols. Garden City, N.Y.: Doubleday, Page, 1926. (Unless otherwise stated, the works below are from the same edition.)
"Autocracy and War."
"Heart of Darkness."
Joseph Conrad: Life and Letters. Edited by G. Jean-Aubruy. 2 vols. Garden City, N.Y.: Doubleday, Page, 1927.
Joseph Conrad's Letters to Cunningham Graham. Edited by C. T. Watts. Cambridge: Cambridge University Press, 1969.
Lord Jim.
Notes on Life and Letters.
A Personal Record.
"Poland Revisited."
"The Secret Sharer."
Under Western Eyes.
Victory.

Vladimir Nabokov

"Fame." In *Poems and Problems*. New York: McGraw-Hill, 1970.
Mary. Translated by Michael Glenny. New York: McGraw-Hill, 1970.

The Nabokov—Wilson Letters. Edited by Simon Karlinski. New York: Harper and Row, 1979.

Nikolai Gogol. Norfolk: New Directions, 1944.

Pale Fire. New York: Berkeley Publishing, 1962.

Pnin. New York: Avon Books, 1969.

The Real Life of Sebastian Knight. New York: New Directions, 1959.

Speak, Memory: An Autobiography Revisited. New York: Putnams, 1966.

Strong Opinions. New York: McGraw-Hill, 1973.

"We So Firmly Believed." In *Poems and Problems.* New York: McGraw-Hill, 1970.

Isaac Bashevis Singer

A Crown of Feathers. Translated by Alma Singer, Herbert Lottman, and others. New York: Farrar, Straus and Giroux, 1973.

A Day of Pleasure. Translated by Joseph Singer, Rosanna Gerber, and others. New York: Farrar, Straus and Giroux, 1969.

Enemies, A Love Story. Translated by Aliza Shervin and Elizabeth Shub. New York: Farrar, Straus and Giroux, 1979.

A Friend of Kafka and Other Stories. Translated by the author and Elizabeth Shub. New York: Farrar, Straus and Giroux, 1979.

Gimpel the Fool and Other Stories. Translated by Saul Bellow, Isaac Rosenfeld, and others. New York: Noonday Press, 1960.

In My Father's Court. Translated by Channah Kleinerman-Goldstein and others. New York: Farrar, Straus and Giroux, 1966.

Old Love and Other Stories. Translated by the author, Joseph Singer, and Elizabeth Shub. New York: Farrar, Straus and Giroux, 1979.

Satan in Goray. Translated by A. H. Gross. New York: Noonday Press, 1955.

Short Friday and Other Stories. Translated by Joseph Singer, Roger Klein, and others. New York: Farrar, Straus and Giroux, 1964.

Shosha. Translated by Joseph Singer and the author. New York: Farrar, Straus and Giroux, 1978.

The Slave. Translated by the author and Cecil Hemley. New York: Farrar, Straus and Giroux, 1979.

A Young Man in Search of Love. Translated by Joseph Singer. New York: Doubleday, 1978.

SECONDARY SOURCES

Alexander, Edward. *Isaac Bashevis Singer.* Boston: Twayne Publishers, 1980.

_____. *The Resonance of Dust: Essays in Holocaust Literature and Jewish Fate.* Columbus: Ohio State University Press, 1979.

Allen, Jerry. *The Sea Years of Joseph Conrad.* Garden City, N.Y.: Doubleday, 1965.

Allentuck, Marcia, ed. *The Achievement of Isaac Bashevis Singer.* Carbondale: Southern Illinois University Press, 1970.

Anderson, Quentin. "Nabokov in Time." *New Republic*, 4 June 1966, pp. 23–28.

Andreach, Robert. "The Two Narrators in 'Amy Foster.'" *Studies in Short Fiction* 11 (Spring 1965):262–69.

Appel, Alfred. "Nabokov's Puppet Show." *New Republic*, 14 January 1967, pp. 23–32.

Appel, Alfred, and Charles Newman, eds. *Nabokov: Criticism, Reminiscences, Translations and Tributes.* Evanston, Ill.: Northwestern University Press, 1970.

Appelfeld, Aharon. "Badenheim 1939." In *New Writings in Israel*, edited by Ezra Spicehandler and Curtis Arnson. Translated by Betty Rosenberg. New York: Schocken Books, 1976.

Baines, Jocelyn. *Joseph Conrad: A Critical Biography.* New York: McGraw-Hill, 1960.

Baron, Solo W. "Medieval Folklore and Jewish Fate." In *Jewish Heritage Reader*, edited by Lily Edelman. Introduction by Morris Aldler. New York: Talinger Publishers, 1965.

Berman, Jeffrey. *Joseph Conrad: Writing as Rescue.* New York: Astra Books, 1977.

Conrad, Jessie. *Joseph Conrad and His Circle.* New York: Dutton, 1935.

Dembo, L. S., ed. *Nabokov: The Man and His Work.* Madison: University of Wisconsin Press, 1967.

Donat, Alexander. "Like Sheep to the Slaughter." In *Out of the Whirlwind*, edited by Albert H. Friedlander. New York: Schocken Books, 1976.

Elman, Richard M. "The Spinoza of Canal Street." *Holiday*, August 1965, pp. 83–87.

Fackenheim, Emil. "The Voice of Auschwitz." In *Modern Jewish Thought*, edited by Nahum N. Glatzer.

Fermi, Laura. *Illustrious Immigrants: The Intellectual Migration from Europe, 1930–1941.* Chicago: University of Chicago Press, 1968.

Field, Andrew. *Nabokov: His Life in Art.* Boston: Little, Brown, 1967.

_____. *Nabokov: His Life in Part.* New York: Viking, 1977.

Fleishman, Avrom. *Conrad's Politics: Community and Anarchy in the Fiction of Joseph Conrad.* Baltimore: Johns Hopkins University Press, 1967.

Fleming, Donald, and Bernard Bailyn, eds. *The Intellectual Migration: Europe and America, 1930–1960.* Cambridge: Harvard University Press, 1969.

Ford, Ford Madox. *Joseph Conrad: A Personal Remembrance.* Boston: Little, Brown, 1924.

Foster, Ludmila A. "Nabokov in Russian Emigre Criticism." In *A Book of Things about Vladimir Nabokov*, edited by Carl R. Proffer. Ann Arbor: Ardis, 1974.

Fowler, Douglas. *Reading Nabokov..* Ithaca: Cornell Unversity Press, 1974.

Frank, M. Z. "The Demon and the Earlock." *Conservative Judaism* (Fall 1965): 1–9.

Geddes, Gary. *Conrad's Later Novels*. Montreal: McGill-Queen's University Press, 1980.

Gekoski, R. A. *Conrad: The Moral World of the Novelist*. London: Elek Books, 1978.

Gillon, Adam. *The Eternal Solitary: A Study of Joseph Conrad*. New York: Bookman Associates, 1960.

Gordon, Ambrose, Jr. "The Double Pnin." In *Nabokov: The Man and His Work*, edited by L. S. Dembo. Madison: University of Wisconsin Press, 1967.

Grabes, H. *Fictitious Biographies: Vladimir Nabokov's English Novels*. The Hague: Mouton, 1977.

Gurko, Leo. *Joseph Conrad: Giant in Exile*. New York: Macmillan, 1962.

Hay, Eloise Knapp. *The Political Novels of Joseph Conrad*. Chicago: University of Chicago Press, 1963.

Hayman, John. "A Conversation with Vladimir Nabokov—with Digressions." *The Twentieth Century* 166 (December 1959):449.

Herndon, Richard. "The Genesis of Conrad's 'Amy Foster.'" *Studies in Philology* 57, no. 3 (1960): 533–66.

Heschel, Abraham Joshua. "The Meaning of This Hour." In *Out of the Whirlwind*, edited by Albert H. Friedlander. New York: Schocken Books, 1976.

Howard, M. "Isaac the Fool." *New Republic*, 21 October 1978, pp. 15–17.

Howe, Irving. "Introduction." In his *Selected Short Stories of Isaac Bashevis Singer*. New York: Modern Library, 1966.

_____. *Politics and Novel*. New York: Avon Books, 1967.

_____. *World of Our Fathers*. New York and London: Harcourt Brace Jovanovich, 1976.

Hughes, Stuart H. *The Sea Changes*. New York: Harper and Row, 1975.

Hyde, G. M. *Vladimir Nabokov: America's Russian Novelist*. London: Marion Boyars, 1977.

Hyman, Stanley Edgar. "The Yiddish Hawthorne." In *On Contemporary Literature*, edited by Richard Kostelanetz. New York: Avon Books, 1964.

Karl. Frederick R. "Jacob Reborn, Zion Regained: I. B. Singer's *The Slave*." In *The Achievements of Isaac Bashevis Singer*, edited by Marcia Allentuck. Carbondale: Southern Illinois University Press, 1970.

_____. *Joseph Conrad: The Three Lives*. New York: Farrar, Straus and Giroux, 1979.

Karlinski, Simon, ed. *The Nabokov–Wilson Letters*. New York: Harper and Row, 1979.

Kazin, Alfred. "The European Writers in Exile." *Jewish Digest* 11 (Summer 1980): 67–75.

_____. "Wisdom in Exile." *New Republic*, 23 July 1977, pp. 12–14.

Khodashevich, Vladislav. "On Sirin." *Tri Quarterly* 5 (Winter 1970): 96–101.

Kogon, Eugen. *The Theory and Practice of Hell*. Translated by Heinz Norded. New York: Berkeley Publishing, 1975.

Kresh, Paul. *Isaac Bashevis Singer: The Magician of West 86th Street*. New York: Dial Press, 1979.

Leavis, F. R. *The Great Tradition: George Eliot, Henry James, Joseph Conrad*. London: Chatto and Windus, 1960.

Lee, L. L. *Vladimir Nabokov*. Boston: Twayne Publishers, 1976.

Madison, Charles A. "I. Bashevis Singer: Novelist of Hasidic Gothicism." In *Yiddish Literature, Its Scope and Major Writers*. New York: Frederick Ungar, 1968.

Malin, Irving, ed. *Critical Views of Isaac Bashevis Singer*. New York: New York University Press, 1969.

Malin, Irving. *Isaac Bashevis Singer*. New York: Frederick Ungar, 1972.

McCarthy, Mary. "A Bolt from the Blue." *New Republic*, 4 June 1962, pp. 21–27.

Meyer, Bernard G. *Joseph Conrad: A Psychoanalytic Biography*. Princeton: Princeton University Press, 1967.

Morf, Gustav. *The Polish Heritage of Joseph Conrad*. London: Sampson, Low, Marston, 1930.

_____. *The Polish Shades and Ghosts of Joseph Conrad*. New York: Astra Books, 1976.

Morrow, L. "The Spiritual World of Isaac Bashevis Singer." *Atlantic*, 24 January 1979, pp. 39–43.

Morton, Donald. *Vladimir Nabokov*. New York: Frederick Ungar, 1974.

Moser, Thomas. *Joseph Conrad: Achievement and Decline*. Cambridge: Harvard University Press, 1960.

Najder, Zdizislaw. *Conrad's Polish Background: Letters to and from Polish Friends*. London: Oxford University Press, 1964.

Nemerov, Howard. *Poetry and Fiction: Essays*. New Brunswick, N.J.: Rutgers University Press, 1963.

Neuman, Franz L. "The Social Science." In *Cultural Migration: The European Scholar in America*. Introduction by W. Rex Crawford. Philadelphia: University of Pennsylvania Press, 1953.

Nicol, Charles. "Pnin's History." *Novel* 4 (Spring 1971): 197–208.

Palmer, John A. *Joseph Conrad's Fiction: A Study in Literary Growth*. Ithaca: Cornell University Press, 1968.

Peretz. I. L. "Bontsha the Silent." In *The Heath Introduction to Fiction*. Introduction and notes by John J. Clayton. Lexington: D.C. Heath, 1977.

Peterson-Kent, Donald. *The Refugee Intellectual: The Americanization of the Immigrants of 1933–1941*. New York: Bookman Associates, 1953.

Pifer, Ellen. *Nabokov and the Novel*. Cambridge: Harvard University Press, 1980.

Proffer, Karl, ed. *A Book of Things about Vladimir Nabokov*. Ann Arbor: Ardis Publishers, 1973.

Quennel, Peter, ed. *Vladimir Nabokov: A Tribute*. New York: William Morrow, 1980.

Quiller-Couch, A. T. "Four Tales by Mr. Conrad." *Bookman* 24(June 1903): 108–9. Rpt. in *Conrad: The Critical Heritage*, edited by Norman Sherry. London and Boston: Routledge and Kegan, 1973.

Reid, Stephen A. "The Unspeakable Rites." In *Conrad: A Collection of Critical Essays*, edited by Marvin Mudrick. Englewood Cliffs, N.J.: Prentice-Hall, 1966.

Roussel, Royal. *The Metaphysics of Darkness*. Baltimore: Johns Hopkins Press, 1971.

Schakovskaya, Zinaida. *V Poiskach Nabokova*. Paris: La Press Libres, 1979.

Seed, D. "The Fiction of Isaac Bashevis Singer." *Critical Quarterly* (Spring 1976): 73–79.

Siegel, Ben. *Isaac Bashevis Singer*. Minneapolis: University of Minnesota Press, 1969.

Sontag, Susan. "Demons and Dreams." *Partisan Review* 29 (Summer 1962): 460–63.

Stegner, Page. *Escape into Aesthetics: The Arts of Vladimir Nabokov*. New York: William Morrow, 1966.

Struve, Gleb. "Nabokov's *Mashenka*." *Times Literary Supplement*, 16 April 1971, p. 449.

Symons, Arthur. *Notes on Joseph Conrad: With Some Unpublished Letters*. 1925; rpt. Freeport, N.Y.: Books for Libraries Press, 1971.

Tanner, Tony. *Conrad: Lord Jim*. London: Edward Arnold, 1963.

Thornburn, David. *Conrad's Romanticism*. New Haven: Yale University Press, 1974.

Trilling, Lionel. "Art and Fortune." In *The Liberal Imagination*. New York: Viking, 1950.

_____. *Beyond Culture*. New York: Viking, 1965.

_____. *The Liberal Imagination*. New York: Viking, 1950.

Wiesenthal, Simon. *The Sunflower*. New York: Schocken Books, 1977.

Wisse, Ruth. "Singer's Paradoxical Progress." *Commentary*, 16 January 1979, pp. 33–38.

Zabieroeski, Stefen. *Conrad in Poland*. Gdansk: WM, 1971.

Index

Alexander, Edward: *Isaac Bashevis Singer*, 78; on *The Slave*, 88

Andreach, Robert J., on Joseph Conrad, 5

Appelfeld, Aharon, "Badenheim 1939," 65

Bailyn, Bernard, and Donald Fleming, eds., *The Intellectual Migration: Europe and America, 1930–1960*, 122

Baron, Solo W., 95

Bobrowski, Tadeusz, 7; and Joseph Conrad, 11

Clifford, Hugh, 10

Conrad, Jessie, 24

Conrad, Joseph, 39, 70, 103, 124; R. J. Andreach on, 5; attitudes toward Germany, 22; attitudes toward Russia, 7–8, 22–23; autobiographical content of writing, 1–2, 4–5, 7, 17; on death, 16, 20–21; and English language, 9–11; on exile, xii, xiv, 4–8, 12–19, 23, 123; exile in life of, xi, xiii–xiv, 7–8, 17, 24, 125; experiences in Africa, 17; experiences at sea, 9; and French language, 8, 11; Gustav Morf on, 3, 22; and lan-

guage, 13–14; motives for writing, 4; and Polish language, 9, 11; A. T. Quiller-Couch, 5; A. Symons on, 2; and writing as communication, 3–4, 20, 23

—work of: "Amy Foster," xiv, 4–6, 8, 12–17, 22; "Autocracy and War," 23; *Congo Diary*, 17; "Falk: A Reminiscence," 5; "Heart of Darkness," 3–4, 17–21; *Lord Jim*, 4–5, 23; *The Nigger of the "Narcissus,"* 5; *A Personal Record*, 2, 9–10; "Poland Revisited," 9; "The Secret Sharer," 3; "Tomorrow," 5; "Typhoon," 5; *Under Western Eyes*, 4, 23–24; *Victory*, 4, 24–26; "Youth," 17

Coulton, G. G., *The Death Penalty for Heresy from 1184 to 1921 A.D.*, 123

Cultural Migration: The European Scholar in America, 122

Exile: as transplantation, xi–xiii, xv, 4, 8, 12, 20–21, 25, 90, 107, 122–26; understanding of, 121–26

Field, Andrew, *Nabokov: His Life in Art*, 30

Fleming, Donald, and Bernard Bailyn, eds., *The Intellectual Mi-*